The New Religion of Life
in Everyday Speech

Don Cupitt

The New Religion of Life in Everyday Speech

SCM PRESS

0 334 02763 2

First published 1999
by SCM Press
9–17 St Albans Place, London N1 0NX

SCM Press is a division of
SCM-Canterbury Press Ltd

Typeset by Regent Typesetting, London
and printed in Great Britain by
Biddles Ltd, Guildford and King's Lynn

For Linda Allen

Contents

Foreword

Ordinary-language, or 'democratic' philosophy has often been discussed during the past half-century, but hardly anyone has ventured to practise it. No doubt people have been influenced by the old assumption that without the controlling influence of academic 'disciplines' and church authorities, the thought of ordinary people must be disorderly, superstitious and lacking in serious intellectual interest.

This essay aims to overthrow that assumption. I collect, analyse and interpret a substantial body of new idioms that have recently become established in the language, with the aim of demonstrating in them a surprisingly coherent, interesting and up-to-date religious philosophy of life. It turns out that ordinary language is the best radical theologian, and significantly sharper than the professionals. Furthermore, establishment in the common language is the most important and powerful kind of establishment there is. I have myself been surprised by what I have discovered, and am left wondering why our contemporary academic philosophy and theology pay so little attention to what is happening in common speech outside the walls. Did not philosophy begin with conversation in the market-place? And surely theologians and preachers need to be more aware that there is modern religious thought, already going on outside the church. It is tougher and better than they might expect: and, in particular, the recent changes in the meaning and use of the word 'life' amount (I think) to a major religious event.

Introduction

An informal shrine on the grass verge by the side of a country road, with flowers and messages. A small hand-painted notice says simply, 'GARY'. People have been visiting and keeping up this little commemorative site for several years now. It marks the very spot where Gary was killed by a car as he cycled along the road.

There are places like this all over Britain nowadays. Some, as at football grounds and at Kensington Palace, have been very spectacular. Others have led to the construction of permanent memorials, such as those in London streets that mark the places where WPC Yvonne Fletcher and Stephen Lawrence fell.

Such rituals have developed only in the past twenty-five years. Typically, they are not connected with conventional religion, or holy ground, or the present site of the body, or the next world. They are popular informal responses to the sudden ending of a *life*. This is the very spot where a dear life prematurely and tragically ebbed away – and so it is the place that people come to in order to remember that life.

Suddenly one realizes how different all this is from attitudes to death in traditional societies. We no longer think about how the dead are getting on, and we are no longer concerned about taking action on their behalf to secure their permanent status in the next world. Instead, we **prefer to remember them as they were in life.** We have come to think that anyone who dies young remains forever young. Memorial services – which began only this century, with the one for Queen Victoria – have gradually become person-centred rather than God-centred. They are described as 'tributes' to the deceased, or as **A Celebration of** the Life of so-and-so. In America, the place of the sermon is commonly taken by a eulogy, or even a discourse addressed to the dead person.

All this is just one indication of an extraordinary religious change that has taken place during the past few decades, as the word 'God' has largely disappeared from common speech, and the old religious language, attitudes, feelings and rituals have increasingly come to be refocused around *life*. I discovered it when I had the idea of collecting all the philosophically and religiously-interesting idioms now current in common speech, and began to notice, first, how many of them are about *life*, and secondly, how closely they are modelled on traditional phrases about and attitudes to God.

This may be the most important religious event of the twentieth century, but it has so far passed almost unnoticed. We have supposed that what has been happening has been *the secularization of religion,* and we have failed to see the much greater event of *the sacralization of life*, even though it has already deeply affected all of us.

How has it happened? I asked a friend, who replied at once: 'The main literary lineage runs from Schopenhauer and Nietzsche through D. H. Lawrence and F. R. Leavis. The later Leavis is full of it.' I don't dispute this: it is obviously correct, at least so far as Britain is concerned. But further discussion and investigation has built up a rather more complex picture of an event that has happened in at least three stages. After Darwin, the philosophies of life and action – Nietzsche, Blondel, Bergson, and American pragmatism. In the 1920s, European philosophy begins to turn to the life-world, to the phenomenology of ordinary life and experience, and to ordinary language – Husserl, Heidegger, Merleau-Ponty, Wittgenstein. At the same time in England, novelists as diverse as Lawrence and Virginia Woolf are highly conscious of the new religious significance of 'life'. But it all becomes fully established in the everyday speech of ordinary people only after the Second World War. The oldest of the new idioms, such as the sanctity of life and you only live once can readily be traced back as far as the 1950s; but others, such as the vivid and forceful **Get a life!** have originated only in the 1990s.

The first indication that 'life' was becoming for ordinary people a new and rather puzzling religious object was the arrival in popular language of the question **What is the meaning of life?** This is a question asked by somebody for whom the old Grand Narratives, the old beliefs in Providence and Progress and future human liberation have broken down. It is a question that was earlier raised – though not quite in so many words – by Shakespeare's tragic heroes, and by Schopenhauer. 'What is the whole tragi-comedy supposed to mean?' But the precise wording I quote – **What is the meaning of life?** – reeks of the mid-1930s in Britain. This is the age of Ogden and Richards's enquiry into *The Meaning of Meaning*, and the beginning of Wittgenstein's lengthy examination of the question: 'What is the meaning of a word?' Old meanings-of-it-all, taken for granted for centuries, are in question; and meaning *itself* is in question. 'Where will it all end?', people ask, because they are no longer convinced by any of the old Big Stories about where history is going, and what hidden purpose is being worked out. 'What's it all in aid of?' Soon the War would shelve such issues for over a decade, a period during which people had little time for speculation. They could see very clearly what had to be done and endured, and why. Then, after the War and in the age of Sartrean Existentialism, the question returns: one friend suggests that high-Sixties protest-and-pop culture simply *was* its full democratization, the moment when people who questioned all traditional authority suddenly saw and asserted that life has no Meaning except the meaning that we give it by our own self-expression.

In terms of cultural history, then, the question, **What is the meaning of life?** has its provenance in the years before and after the Second World War – the epoch of phenomenology and existentialism. It is the age when 'life', *this* life, is being discovered by ordinary people as a challenge and a puzzle. (In more recent years, **This Life** has even become the title of a television series.) Various British philosophers of the Fifties and

Sixties, such as R. W. Hepburn and Karl Britton, wrote essays and books about **The Meaning of Life** in response to this popular questioning, but I think none of them wrote about what was happening to the meaning of 'life', the *word*. And that, I suggest, is the real issue and the big novelty: the word 'life' is changing its meaning and becoming religiously-charged, in a way that certain writers such as Thoreau, Nietzsche and Lawrence anticipated. This change is hard to see and describe, even today: but it's a much greater change than people have yet realized. It seems that the object of religious concern and attention is no longer something hoped-for after death or at the end of history, but something that gives itself to us, and in which we are immersed, in the here and now: life. There is a corresponding ethical shift away from rule-morality and the service of a great historically-unfolding Purpose, towards an expressionist ethic of **lifestyle**, coming out and doing one's own thing in one's own way.

I have been led to this topic by two or three lines of enquiry. I have already mentioned the fact that I have been collecting (with help from some friends such as Bernard Brown) philo-sophically-interesting idioms from common speech. I had a crazy idea of making the philosophy of religion a sort-of empiri-cal subject – even a popular subject, even in Britain! We found, of course, that 'life' is the subject of many new sayings. (Phrases heard, noted down, and now used in this book as being new and relevant to its argument, are printed in **bold** type.) This in turn reminded me of the nineteenth-century unbeliever's turn to 'life', reading Schopenhauer anthologies with titles like *The Wisdom of Life*, and quoting Spinoza's saying that the wise man meditates not about death, but about life. Perhaps, when traditional religious objects and forms of action fade away, frustrated religious feeling is displaced onto 'life' – *this* life.

> O look, look in the mirror,
>   O look in your distress;
> Life remains a blessing
>   Although you cannot bless.

Secondly, after the two books about Being, I asked myself how far ideas like the ones I was expounding are already part of ordinary people's consciousness. I quickly decided that they are; but where Heidegger put Being, ordinary language prefers to put Life. For ordinary people the great event has been a dramatic revaluation of this life, doubtless connected in Britain with events like the foundation of the National Health Service and the great humanitarian charities, and perhaps also with their visits to the military cemeteries in France and Belgium.

The rapid progress and great expansion of medical science since the Second World War could hardly fail to attract religious interest. People use religious language in connection with the *devotion* to patient care of many doctors, nurses and paramedics; in connection with the *wonders* or *miracles* of modern medicine; and perhaps most of all in connection with the *free gift* of blood and other organs **to save lives**. People who have lost a close relative, perhaps a child, speak of the comfort they have gained **from the knowledge that by her death she was able to give life to others**. The echo of traditional Christian language is umistakeable.

A further preliminary clue: the rise of the modern historical consciousness, of psychology, and of the novel has obliged people to try to imagine the human life and even the human personality of Jesus in a way that was never attempted by the older tradition. Similarly, the same factors, plus the new nineteenth-century ideas about development, about social theory and about biological evolution have obliged people at large to think about *life itself* in a way they very rarely did before. We have come to recognize the extent to which our existence is *situated*, biologically, socially, historically. In the older tradition, humans were first and foremost *mortals*, destined for death. Life was something that belonged as of right only to the gods and the next world, something that you might hope to participate in by Grace in this world and permanently in the 'hereafter'. Out of this background a religious outlook developed that concentrated on preparation for the next and better world, and never really got round to finding out what it is to be a human

animal, a living organism, already *in life* and **with a life to live**
here and now. It is not surprising that we could end up oddly
alienated from life, and not surprising that the admirably brutal
(note the word) injunction **Get a life!** has become such a popular idiom in these past few years. **I just want to get my life
together again**, people say: **I want to get back to living a normal
life. Life must go on**: it's become the first imperative. One must
keep up with life, and play one's full part in it.

When I quoted to a friend the tribute-phrase **She loved life**,
and declared that only very recently has it become possible to
praise the dead in such language, he quoted Jonathan Swift. I
looked – and found this:

> Although reason were intended by providence to govern our
> passions, yet it seems in two points of the greatest moment to
> the being and continuance of the world, God hath intended
> our passions to prevail over reason. The first is, the propaga-
> tion of our species, since no wise man ever married from the
> dictates of reason. The other is, **the love of life**, which, from
> the dictates of reason, every man would despise, and wish it
> at an end, or that it never had a beginning.
>
> *Thoughts on Religion*, 15[1] (my bold type)

Jonathan Swift (1667-1745), Dean of St Patrick's, Dublin, was
an orthodox churchman and still remains a hero in Ireland for
his championing of the cause of the Irish people. He was a
philanthropist; yet he regards this life of ours as being, from
the point of view of reason, despicable. It is not intrinsically
interesting or valuable. It is worthless or worse: rationally, one
should wish oneself dead or unborn. As for the pleasure we
take in life or in sex, it too is worthless in itself: it is a mere non-
rational sweetener, added by God to make our plight less
unbearable and keep us going.

Although he lived well into the years of the Enlightenment,
Swift – here at least – is found to retain intact the old savage
pessimism that had largely prevailed since late antiquity. His
view of life or **perspective upon life** is in many ways the
opposite of ours, for we live in a totally different era in which

phrases such as **the worth of life, the value of life, the sanctity of life,** and **quality of life** have recently become widely current. **Quality of life** has become such an accepted idiom that decision-makers in medicine and the para-medical professions even *quantify* it, in 'qualys', so that one can compare the relative worth of different states of life under different degrees of disadvantage and disability. **Quality-adjusted life-years** have become part of the health economist's currency: indeed, for public officials **quality of life**, together with **right to life**, is now the most general unit of ethical assessment.

More recently, we have learnt to go well beyond the prudent utilitarian calculation of quality-adjusted life-years. Our *joie de vivre* may run so high that it leads us recklessly to tempt life, just as in the Bible men sometimes *tempted God* and in the older English idiom they *tempted fate*. Our new idioms for this are the Nietzschean *'live dangerously'* and the popular phrases **live fast, die young, living on the edge** and **live hard,** an amusing variant on *diehard*.

This is a whole world of thought of which Swift knew nothing, and we cannot excuse or explain his **despair of life** – or, if you prefer, his **sin against life** – by referring to the severe psychological troubles that afflicted him in his last years. Today, similarly afflicted people and others perhaps even worse troubled often respond by loving and extolling life only the more ardently. As life begins to slip away from us a little, we see how precious it is. We no longer accept Death's old cry that

Life is an oyster with nothing inside it;
  Not to be born is the best for man . . .

We are learning to love life *disinterestedly*. It is only the flux of things, pouring out and slipping away, slipping away from us. But **it means the world to us.** Life's meaning is – life itself. And that is the new religious relation to life. In the old order religion preached to us the vanity of this life and the certainty of death in order to awaken our desire for a very different and unpoisoned post-mortem life. Thus the way to eternal life beyond the grave was by spending the present era busily preparing for death. In Catholic Christian spirituality all the attention and the value was concentrated upon 'the inner life', or 'the interior life' of the soul with God, and one's 'outward' this-worldly life with others was relatively neglected. Swift himself in his best moments could see the absurdity of this:

> Very few men, properly speaking, live at present, but are providing to live another time.[2]

In the new order now coming into being, religion is seen as teaching us to live at present. It consists in learning to love life in a fully-disinterested and solar (unreserved, ardent) way in the here-and-now. A solar love of life has already conquered death, and is therefore already eternal life. So you can have 'eternal life' right now: it is just a certain way of loving and living this life.

It is of course the central idea of St John's Gospel that the believer who participates by faith in the divine life possesses eternal life in the here and now (e.g., John 3.36, 5.24, 6.47, 6.54).[3] In our own new age of religious naturalism, we find just the same eternal joy through solar love of this life, now. **That's what life's all about.**

* * *

When, a generation ago, the Franks Commission was mulling over the perennial question of whether the University of Oxford can or should ever be reformed, a Commissioner suggested to a witness that the College system was surely a good thing, because all those great minds could cross-fertilize each other over the High Table. 'Well, no', came the reply: 'Actually, it's considered rather bad form to talk shop'.

Cambridge is happily different. I have received immediate replies to my queries about matters of language and literature from John Harvey, John Beer, Glen Cavaliero, Robert Douglas-Fairhurst, Peter Burke and many others. Thanks also to Steven Shakespeare, Gavin Hyman, Hugh Rayment-Pickard, Petra Green and other readers of drafts. A further debt of many years' standing is acknowledged in the dedication.

Cambridge, 1999

I

A New Meaning of 'Life'

During the nineteenth century in Europe the old power of the Church, the sacred world and religious doctrine was steadily weakening, whilst at the same time the world of secular life and culture was expanding very rapidly. New fields were being opened up and colonized, one after another. In these newly-established territories there was a strong demand for suitable vocabulary, idioms, standard patterns of thinking and institutional structures. Quite simply, all these things were needed in order to *develop* the new territories.

Inevitably, the old country – that is, the Church – was called upon to supply the necessary materials. Religious language, attitudes and patterns of thinking were exported from the sacred realm, and refocused around the new ideas about, for example, national identity, political allegiance and art. The Church had always seen itself as the *plebs sancta dei*, the holy common people of God, filled with one Spirit and buoyed up by the promise of a glorious destiny. The Church's feeling for the way to maintain communal identity through adversity and over the centuries, the Church's interesting combination of populism and élite government, the Church's messianic self-image and sense of destiny – all this was exactly what emergent nationalisms required. They seized it gratefully, and nationalism accordingly developed as a kind of displaced or *émigré* religiosity.

A point often missed in this connection is that when people abandon traditional religious allegiance, they do not suddenly stop using religious language, having religious feelings, and thinking in religious ways. Far from it: all these things remain, but frustrated now and urgently seeking a fresh love-object. When they find it, they will latch on to it fiercely. So the new sense of one's ethnic or national identity was quickly found to be – or perhaps rather, was made into – the perfect replacement for one's former but now failing sense of religious identity.

Political parties further illustrate the extraordinary extent to which Western institutions have continued to be modelled on the Church, and still to this day like to describe their structure, their working and their problems in religious metaphors. Manifestos were modelled on creeds and confessions, political leaders upon charismatic preachers, and working-class solidarity upon the priesthood of all believers. Abhorrence and fear of factionalism and schism passed from church and chapel to party: the party is of course a broad church, people say, but in New Labour all members of the PLP 'are expected to sing from the same hymn-sheet'.

A similar amused awareness of the extent to which every Western institution betrays its religious origins inspired George Bernard Shaw's observation that 'All professions are conspiracies against the laity'.[1] During the nineteenth century the new upwardly-mobile professions – and, above all, the medical profession – actively borrowed from the clergy even while the clergy themselves were beginning to decline. Copying the clergy, the newer professions learnt the value of being discreet, unctuous and reassuring advisors; they learnt to talk jargon amongst themselves, and to talk *down* to the laity. Every profession and branch of knowledge became a sort of Church, with its own high priesthood. In every case there developed an Establishment – that is, a governing professional body that supervises entry to the profession, sets and enforces standards, and defines the limits of orthodox doctrine. Even to this day, professions such as psychotherapy that (as yet) lack the proper ecclesiastically-modelled control of truth and style of government are considered to lack respectability. The old Church itself may not be any longer much respected, but anyone *else* who seeks to win respect has got to get organised like a church.

Writers and artists joined in all this: but they, instead of being assimilated to the priestly and institutional strand in religion, more usually adopted the role of the charismatic prophet. Nineteenth-century leaders of opinion such as Carlyle, Ruskin and Arnold in Britain, or Lowell, Emerson and William James in America, wrote in the manner of somewhat heterodox liberal clergymen and published volumes of what they might openly describe as *Lay Sermons*. This type of writer was successively liberal cleric, 'prophet', cultural guide, critic and (today) a 'critical theorist'.

Painters found themselves caught up in a framework of understanding that was nationalist and historicist. Art historians defined the various national schools, and the various newly-established National Galleries arranged their collections accordingly. Each country's line of painters was then seen as having made the same sort of contribution to their nation's history as Israel's line of canonical prophets had made to ancient Jewish history. The European national picture-gallery came to be laid out as a hushed temple in which one communed with the national spirit through the works of its greatest prophets. In the same way each European country needed (and most of them found) a national composer whose symphonies and tone poems captured the spirit of the country's folk culture and landscape.

The biblical picture of the prophet as the barometer of his age, a suffering, misunderstood and persecuted figure who is vindicated and canonized only posthumously, was adopted enthusiastically by nineteenth-century artists, as everyone knows. What is not so often noticed is that the old archetype remains very potent even today, for in today's 'performance' and 'conceptual' art we see an almost uncannily exact echo and repetition of the eccentric behaviour and symbolic prophecies of the biblical Ezekiel. Damien Hirst: our Ezekiel, with the same mortuary preoccupations.

I am making the paradoxical observation that it is only in a period of religious disintegration that we see really clearly how prodigiously powerful, and perhaps ineradicable, are religious ways of thinking and behaving. In a period of secularization religious language does not die out: what happens is that as the centre weakens, the fringe gets bigger. The old mainstream uses of religious language weaken and are forgotten, but – as in the case, for example, of words like *miracle* and *revelation* – extended, metaphorical uses proliferate unchecked, spreading out across **the life-world**.

To this day, when scientists seek to communicate their ideas to the general public, they do so by putting on religious dress – assuming the manner of high priests or seers, borrowing religious vocabulary, speaking with evangelical conviction, and presenting the current consensus of the scientific conversation as if it were timeless 'gospel truth'. (Notice that old, out-of-date science books are hopelessly bad, dead and dull in just the same way, and for the same reasons, as old theology books.) The paradox is that although today natural science is at the top and theology at the very bottom of the cultural pecking-order, there remains a sense in which theology is *still* the queen of the sciences and the Church is still the central institution of the West. All Western institutions, professions and knowledge-systems remain profoundly influenced by the religious social structures and ways of thinking that cradled them.

This background may serve to introduce an aspect of secularization that has as yet been little discussed. Quite recently – I believe, only in the past 30 or 40 years – it has become very noticeable that in common speech much of the old vocabulary in which people used to express their relation to God has been transferred to 'life'. As the hope of post-mortem personal salvation has become less vivid, the focus of religious concern and religious feeling has been brought forward into this life – that is, our present biological and social life – in a way that affects Christians too. **We believe in life** *before* **death**, says the Christian Aid poster, a slogan that invites abridgement: **We believe in life**. Paradoxically, the secularization of religion has had the effect of sacralizing life.

In this new religious world, your personal happiness and your hope of salvation, your *wholeness*, depends not upon faith in things invisible but upon your **attitude to life**. For example, when someone has died young and we are looking for words, we may say of her that **she loved life**.[2] When I quoted this to another colleague (I have tried out these ideas on many long-suffering friends), he raised his eyebrows: 'What's "life"? And what is it to *love* life? Do we know?' My reply is obvious: 'At least we *do* know that to say that **she loved life** is now an entirely acceptable thing to say about her, whereas if we were to say that she loved *God* there would follow an embarrassed silence. In fact today there are over 140 religious idioms in which we can talk about life, about **where it is leading us**, where it is **carrying us**, what **lessons it is teaching us** and **how it is treating us**, and about our own attitudes in response – attitudes of **gratefulness to life**, of **unworthiness to live**, of resignation to **life's apparent unfairness**, and perhaps also of **distrust and despair of life** – and all these idioms and attitudes are now daily voiced and expressed in association with *life*, whereas their old association with *God* has suddenly and simply dropped out of living speech. Mysteriously, nobody now seems to know any longer what it is or was *to love God*; but everyone seems to understand what it is **to love life**. In common speech and on the media we almost daily hear it said that **all life is sacred**; we hear talk of **the sanctity of life** and of **reverence** or **respect for life**, and we may hear quoted William Blake's '*Everything that lives is holy*': but when did you last hear the holiness or sacredness of *God* invoked seriously in everyday conversation?

Any answer to that last question must recall public debates in the fairly recent past about Sunday observance and about the blasphemy laws. Originally, you were supposed to keep Sunday holy because God was holy; but nowadays not even the Sabbatarians would try to use that argument. Instead, they can only urge us to keep Sunday special for the sake of our own well-being (but note that all this applies only so far as Sabbatarians still exist at all). As for the blasphemy laws, if they are defended it is not on the grounds that to blaspheme against the holiness of God is to invite crushing divine retribution, but on the humanistic and utilitarian grounds that it is cruel and wrong deliberately to hurt the feelings of religious people. So today, for all practical purposes life is sacred, but God isn't any more. We often hear talk of **a crime against life, a sin against life, a blasphemy against life**; but we rarely hear talk of these offences against *God*. So far as common speech is concerned, virtually the whole of our surviving language about God, the things of God and our relation to God has been comprehensively demythologized and brought down into this relatively novel entity called life. We want and expect to find religious value here and now, in this life. If we are not finding it, we protest: **Is this it? Surely there's more to life than this? This can't be all there is to it.**

And yet nobody's talking about the shift and its implications. In the great dictionaries of English, French and German the entries under the words life, living, *leben, lebens-* and *vie* are very long, listing eight or more major patterns of use and hundreds of idioms. But they do not single out for attention the group of uses to which I am drawing attention – that is, the uses of 'life' to signify a thing or power or agency that carries us along as a fast-flowing river carries a boat, this way and that; a moving Power that is both immanent within us and (poetically) over against us or surrounding us, that is thought of as not only filling us and inspiring us, but also as having quasi-personal attributes; as **treating us well** or **badly**, as **teaching** us (because there is, of course, a **university of life**), as **having things in store for us** and so on: and therefore as being the proper object of religious attitudes on our part. For example, on 29 September 1922 D. H. Lawrence wrote to Catherine Carswell commending **a gentle faith in life itself**.[3] And for a second and more recent example, F. R. Leavis, writing in 1975 about T. S. Eliot's *Four Quartets*, uses such phrases as **fear of life** and **sin against life**.[4] Lawrence and Leavis (especially the later Leavis) have indeed been very influential in spreading the new ways of speaking about life through the culture – but the dictionaries seem not as yet to be recording it. I believe the reason is that whereas the literary pedigree of the new religious notion of life is very ancient, it has entered into common speech, and has settled down into stock idioms such as dictionaries record, only in very recent years. Perhaps, since 'life' is one of the toughest words in the book, and lexicographers are conservative folk, they have been reluctant to notice such a momentous shift in speech. They scarcely even record the sort of use of 'life' by Lawrence and Leavis that I have mentioned. (Nor do they record the extent to which the place of religion in people's lives has been taken since the 1960s by a rather new entity called 'culture'. It is, for example, their 'culture' which nowadays impels members of the Orange Order to put on their regalia and march through Catholic neighbourhoods in Northern Ireland. Even Protestant-ism is no longer religion; it has been demythologized into 'culture'.)

I suspect that most of the interested parties have reason not to observe the shift I am describing. Professional theologians, for example, will not rejoice to hear that ordinary language is generations ahead of them theologically; and the more con-servative church members may be upset by the suggestion that the common speech they daily use now has implicit in it a new secular religion, rather different from the old religion that they still profess with their lips on Sundays. What they would dis-approvingly describe as 'radical theology' has conquered by stealth, quietly becoming built into our everyday speech without our being aware of it.

It can happen, of course, that the shift is delicate enough to pass unnoticed. Expecting imminent judgment or death, believers used to be told to 'live each day as if thy last': we should be vigilant, because the end will come suddenly like a thief in the night. Translating that injunction into a modern idiom, there is amongst us a tacit consensus that since we know that death may indeed come at any time, but is nothing and therefore cannot be prepared for, the only way to prepare for death is to say (out loud, now): 'We should **live life to the full.** Since I passed sixty I have **taken life as it comes, one day at a time, as a gift**, a bonus. I'm **grateful – to life, for life**, while it lasts.'[5] So we do still, like our forebears, live each day aware of the gratuitousness of Being, aware of life's brevity and fragility, and so aware that each day may indeed be our last. The shift has indeed occurred, we know damned well that it has occurred, and it is massive. *But it is also delicate*, and many of the people I know find it convenient to be able to play it down and not draw attention to it. What comes after death used to be infinitely great and terrible, whereas now it is, very simply, nothing. But because both of these post-mortem states are quite incommensurable with the daily process of life as we now live it, their effect in the language is rather similar. Either way, think short-term and don't plan too far ahead. Either way, **love life while you have it**. Life's a pure gift with no giver: it comes undeserved, and we never get to earn or own it. That's *real* Grace, utterly gratuitous. Make the best of the time you're given. As the New Testament writer admirably puts it: 'While we have time, let us do good unto all men . . .'[6]

Do you see? Whether life is dominated by eschatological expectation, as in early Christianity, or whether death is simply the end of life, as today, the ethical injunction comes out pretty much the same. Indeed, the deep religious continuity between Christianity and post-Christianity comes out very clearly in the new popular idioms. **Make the most of the time you have left**, people say: **Live life to the full**. Best of all, keep repeating the lovely, duplicitous phrase: **Have the time of your life**, as I recently found myself saying to a friend who has been told that he has only a few months left. Now *there* is a truly beautiful post-Christian preparation for death: 'I am resolved that the time I have left, the remaining time of my life, shall be *the time of my life*!' So the thought of the nothingness of death precipitates one into a passionate love of life, time, lifetime and life's time. As I get old, I am turning into a mayfly; I'm becoming *daily more ephemeral*.[7] As the prospect before one gets shorter and shorter, life becomes sweeter and sweeter. The more short-term your vision, the more intense becomes your feeling for life.

Our doctrinal conservatism and nostalgia are preventing us from seeing the profound implications of the linguistic changes that have already taken place, as God has been brought down into, and dispersed into life. Religious ways of thinking and the religious form of life are so powerful and persistent that they *easily* survive even the total disappearance of the old doctrinal and metaphysical superstructure. So the new religion – or the next phase of the old religion, if you prefer – is already taking shape amongst us. And it arrives, not by revelation, nor by some clever person's instruction, but in a democratic and populist way as we all gradually become aware of the implications of idioms we have already begun to use. **That's life.**

Put it another way: before the Enlightenment, the human being was thought of as having been inserted naked into a ready-made cosmos with an inbuilt rational and moral order. Naked, one was confronted by certain great theological, moral and cosmic facts, necessities and claims. Think how religious art always depicted the human being, both in the very beginning in Eden and at our last End on Judgement Day, as *naked*.

The new situation, as people begin to understand it after the French Revolution, replaces the cosmos and the old Last Things with a new object called 'life'. It is the human life-world, it is 'the flow', it is history, language and culture, it is All This around us. And in it, we are by no means naked: we are always already **in the land of the living**, we already belong to a language-group and inherit a culture. We join a conversation that is already going on. We are not just *in* life; 'life' is *us*, all of us.

In a word, then: we used to be naked, confronted by all the ultimates. Now, we are like the characters in a soap opera, always already immersed in life. Only very recently have we begun to grasp the sheer magnitude of the change. Nietzsche announced the Death of God to a still-baffled public, a hundred years or so after it had actually happened: today one might say that the coming of this new thing called 'life' is being announced and understood *two centuries* in arrears – and *still* it's mystifying.

Genealogies of 'Life'

I have said that the new meaning of life, though it has become established in the idioms of common speech only in the past 30 years or so, has a very ancient literary pedigree. But all genealogies are more or less fictitious, and I am certainly not going to suggest that there is One True Story about where and when the new meaning of 'life' began and how it has become established. Instead, I shall briefly set out *three* stories, one behind another.

Consider, to begin with, the following four texts. The first is from D. H. Lawrence, towards the end of his life, writing from the Mediterranean to Charles Wilson back in England. He's commenting upon newspaper reports about the current industrial unrest:

> It's time there was an *enormous* revolution – not to instal soviets, but to give life itself a chance. What's the good of an industrial system piling up rubbish, while nobody lives. We want a revolution not in the name of money or work or any of that, but of life – and let money and work be as casual in human life as they are in a bird's life, damn it all . . . The dead materialism of Marx socialism and soviets seems to me no better than what we've got. What we want is life and *trust*; men trusting men, and making living a free thing, not a thing to be *earned*. But if men trusted men, we could soon have a new world . . .[1]

We would need a Lawrence concordance and a full-scale academic study of his very rich and varied use of the word 'life' to do justice to this text, but three or four strands of influence upon its wording are immediately obvious. There is here the old Romantic Schiller-and-Wordsworth argument that a human being is a living, growing creature, who is being horribly warped and diminished by being caged within a minutely-regulated commercial and industrial system. There are strong echoes of the Bible, especially of the birds in the Sermon on the Mount, and of the kind of utopian radical protestantism best known to most people now through William Blake. And in his naturalism and vitalism, and his association of 'life' with freedom, creativity and magnanimity, Lawrence everywhere shows the influence of Nietzsche. Ignore the rather-deplorable racial generalizations, and consider the language:

> (The aboriginal peoples in Mexico were) people who never really changed. Men who were not faithful to life, to the living actuality. Faithful (instead, merely) to some dark necessity out of the past . . .[2]

> The Spaniards I believe, have refused life so long that life now refuses them, and they are rancid.[3]

To get clearer about what Lawrence is saying in his talk of life, consider how his message about being faithful to life differs from the more familiar injunction, 'To thine own self be true', from *Hamlet*. This is the voice of Renaissance moral individualism, no doubt, but one wouldn't wish to say that it recommended *a religious attitude to one's own self*: whereas Lawrence does clearly and invariably recommend **a religious attitude to life**. In *The Plumed Serpent* (1926, c.xxii), for example, we find the injunction to 'seek life' four times on one page, and twice in such terms as to make it unmistakably clear that Lawrence is deliberately echoing and rewriting biblical texts. He writes:

> . . . seek life where it is to be found . . .
> . . . seek life first
> . . . seek life, and life will bring the change . . .
> . . . seek life itself[4]

The first of these is evidently a variant upon Isaiah 55.6, 'Seek the Lord while he may be found' and the second rewrites the Sermon on the Mount: 'Seek ye first the Kingdom of God . . .' (Matthew 6.33). Lawrence is putting 'life' where religious tradition puts the word 'God', and the relation to life where tradition puts the relation to God. *Exactly* as Jesus says, put God first, and then everything else will be added, so Lawrence repeatedly says that the one thing needful is that we learn to put life first, and then everything else will sort itself out.

A second example of the extent to which Lawrence's life-talk parallels the theologians: in *Kangaroo* (1923) he runs oddly close to Martin Buber's existentialist account of God and God's relation to the soul – even though, surprisingly, Buber's *I and Thou* was first published in German only in the same year. We don't have descriptive knowledge of either life or God. We know them only by listening to and answering their call to us:

> Life makes no absolute statement. It is all Call and
> Answer . . . (*Kangaroo*, c.13; Penguin Books edn., p.295).

I think it is correct to say that in this passage Lawrence is inventing what would come to be called 'existentialism', *independently*.

Seventy years after Lawrence's death, we have gone a long way towards implementing his programme. Consider, for example, how when a modern person is in despair and distress we say not, 'You must repent and change your relation to God', but 'You need to change your whole attitude to life'. 'Cognitive therapy' fits neatly into the slot formerly occupied by *metanoia*, repentance.

Again, we used to say to the same distressed person that faith goes on believing in the goodness and love of God however bad things get to be. Sometimes God's face seems to smile on us, sometimes it seems to be dark; but even in the darkest times faith believes that behind the clouds God's face is still shining. And this old recognition of the ambivalence of the believer's experience is continued in our modern life-talk. Life, too, has a bright side and a dark side: **Always look on the bright side of life.**

Now a second text, from the year 1854. Henry David Thoreau describes 'What I lived for' at Walden:

> I went to the woods because I wished to live deliberately, to front only the essential facts of life, and see if I could not learn what it had to teach, and not, when I came to die, discover that I had not lived. I did not wish to live what was not life, living is so dear; nor did I wish to practice resignation, unless it was quite necessary. I wanted to live deep and suck out all the marrow of life, to live so sturdily and Spartanlike as to put to rout all that was not life, to cut a broad swath and cut close, to drive life into a corner, and reduce it to its lowest terms, and, if it proved to be mean, why then to get the whole and genuine meanness of it, and publish its meanness to the world; or if it were sublime, to know it by experience, and be able to give a true account of it in my next excursion. For most men, it appears to me, are in a strange uncertainty about it (sc., life), whether it is of the devil or of God, and have *somewhat hastily* concluded that it is the chief end of man here to 'glorify God and enjoy him for ever'.[5]

Along with *Moby Dick* (1851), *Walden* is generally regarded as one of the books in which American literature at last finds its own true American voice. It is clear straightaway that Thoreau is not going to live alone in the wilderness for any of the Old World's traditional reasons. He's not going into the desert like Elijah or Muhammad to listen out for the voice of God; he's not going like Jesus or Anthony to be tempted of the devil; and he's not going, like Wittgenstein or Kerouac, in order to seek relief for his own troubled psychology. He's going to try to find out for himself what it is to be a human being with **a life to live** – something that, as he suggests with more than a hint of sarcasm, the old religious tradition has mysteriously neglected to tell us. Our religion was so preoccupied with warning us about our imminent Final Examination, and teaching us how to prepare for it so that we would reach at least the pass standard and so gain our place in the next life, that it entirely distracted us from discovering what *this* life is. We are strangely ignorant of it:

Still we live meanly, like ants . . . Our life is frittered away by
detail . . . Why should we live with such hurry and waste of
life? . . . Simplify, simplify, simplify![6]

Thoreau's spirituality of simple living is his new version of
monasticism. One lives simply in order to attend to life and
learn to see it face to face, like God. In his own very different
way, Thoreau is as keen as Lawrence to pull religious metaphors back down into the life from which they were originally
taken. For example, in religion someone waiting for the Coming
of God or the Second Advent of Christ was traditionally
portrayed as being like someone waiting through the night for
dawn to come. But Thoreau reverses the movement and brings
the religious metaphor back into our daily experience. When we
are fully awakened, *ordinary* life is 'poetic or divine life':

We must learn to reawaken and keep ourselves awake, not by
mechanical aids, but by an infinite expectation of the dawn,
which does not forsake us in our soundest sleep.[7]

Thoreau wants us to be so attuned to life that we sleep
soundly every night, warm in our Advent Hope or 'infinite
expectation' of dawn. Here he reminds us of a general point: as
in the past 150 years people have battled to discover 'life', wanting to know what it is and how to live it, so there have arisen a
wide range of movements that seek to 'close the gap': the gap
between Art and Life, between Literature and Life, between
Religion and Life. The aim seems to be to recover a long-lost
primal unity, an intensity of lived experience in which everything was poetic, everything was divine:

In the earliest times . . . there can have existed no division
between the poetic and the prosaic. Everything must have
been tinged with magic. Thor was not the god of thunder; he
was the thunder and the god.

For a true poet, every moment of existence, every act,
ought to be poetic since, in essence, it is so. As far as I know,
no one to this day has attained that high state of awareness.
Browning and Blake got closer to it than anyone else.[8]

So Borges, in a Preface to *The Gold of the Tigers*, datelined 'Buenos Aires, 1972', and one may well wish to argue with him about just which artists have left us enough evidence to judge that they nearly reached the top. Blake – yes, indeed; but why *Browning*? However that may be, I have argued elsewhere that 'the top' (i.e., the highest that is accessible to a human being) is eternal joy in the efflux of pure contingency – i.e., in *life*. And for passages to illustrate it I have elsewhere suggested texts by Dōgen and, above all, Eckhart, to whom we turn again now for our third text. Eckhart, with his usual dazzling ease and wit, ascribes to life the most fundamental of all God's attributes, *aseity* or from-himself-ness. Like God, life is self-grounding. It just affirms itself. It needs no reason:

> If anyone went on for a thousand years asking of life: "Why are you living?", life, if it could answer, would only say: "I live so that I may live." That is because life lives out of its own ground and springs from its own source, and so it lives without asking itself why it is living.[9]

Eckhart (c.1260-1327), after a lengthy scholastic education, was active during the first quarter of the fourteenth century. He lived under conditions that were, to put it bluntly, absolutely *mediaeval*. How does he contrive to be so astonishingly, anachronistically, bright? He speaks of life as something like a well-spring or fountain that springs up spontaneously, and joyfully affirms itself. It is a divine *élan vital* that courses through us, vitalizing us as it affirms itself in us. Where can Eckhart have learnt all this?

Partly, surely, from his use in preaching of the German vernacular, with its very rich and *lebenslustig* stock of compound words related to life. He is a writer; and if you are a writer, language itself gives you your ideas. But it is also worth recalling that in antiquity, and therefore also in the Bible, what we just called 'the gap' between Religion and Life – that is, the gap between the vocabulary of religion and the vocabulary of the life-world – was nothing like so wide as it is today. Thor was once the thunder *and* the god *undividedly*, and similarly, in the

Bible words like *breath, wind, spirit, God, life,* and *Christ* could run very close together in the same sentences without any feeling of incongruity. On the Day of Pentecost, the 'rushing mighty wind' simply *is* the Divine Spirit. What today people call **the kiss of life** (resuscitation) was once the same thing as the Gift of the Spirit. The prophet Elisha, in the Bible, gives the kiss of life to a child, much like a modern ambulanceman (II Kings, 4.34). Resuscitation *was* resurrection. Spirit *was* wind or breath: breathing your last *was* giving up the ghost. In the Fourth Gospel the terms 'life' and 'eternal life' are used interchangeably in a way that, by our standards, comes near to equating *all* life with the divine life. In which case the recent discovery in ordinary language of the sacredness of 'life' and 'breath' is arguably, and to some extent, a *re*discovery of what our religious tradition once meant. Notice, in this connexion, what a strong and ancient religious word we use in connection with the contamination of air or water – *pollution*. So far as we can, we ought to see *everything* as holy, and not 'defile' anything.

Finally, a fourth text, from the conversation of Gilgamesh with the woman winemaker Siduri. The death of his friend Enkidu has brought home to Gilgamesh the Information that he is mortal. Afraid of death, he resolves to set out on a quest for immortality. Siduri scoffs:

> She answered, 'Gilgamesh, where are you hurrying to? You will never find that life for which you are looking. When the gods created man they allotted to him death, but life they retained in their own keeping. As for you, Gilgamesh, fill your belly with good things; day and night, night and day, dance and be merry, feast and rejoice. Let your clothes be fresh, bathe yourself in water, cherish the little child that holds your hand, and make your wife happy in your embrace; for this too is the lot of man.'[10]

In a great deal of Bronze Age thought – and especially in Mesopotamia – life and death are not so much present conditions or states of being, but *fates*. That is to say that men are mortals, and only gods and spirits are immortal. They are down for life, and we are down for death. A breath of life from them in their world may come down and cause a temporary stir in this world, but the fact remains that everything in this world gravitates steadily towards death and dissolution. As the Christian poet says:

> Successive nights like rolling waves,
> Carry them forward, who are bound for death.

For thousands of years the basic cliché about human beings was not that we are alive, but that 'All men are mortal'. This must be one reason why the discovery of 'life' – like the discovery of the body, the self, the imagination, and human psychology – is essentially modern, and indeed rather Late Modern. This suggests a really dandy hypothesis: we may be able to see the whole history of Being, from the early Bronze Age to the present day, as a very gradual coming back to life. Bit by bit, eternal life and eternal joy in life are returned into the human realm and there naturalized. The end of the process is the discovery of 'life' in the new and now fully-human sense. God dies, man comes back to life, eternal life comes back to humans.

Just occasionally one finds in a writer something that seems to mark a decisive step in this long process. Wordsworth's line, 'The pleasure which there is in life itself', from 'Michael', l.77, is an example. Here Wordsworth seems to be the first great figure in the old mainstream tradition of Christian Platonism who, quite straightforwardly and without embarrassment or apology, can speak of this natural life of ours and of sense-experience as being intrinsically good and pleasurable. Indeed, a completely innocent and serious use of the word 'pleasure' is characteristic of his writing. He can even sound, as in 'Tintern Abbey', l.27, almost Nietzschean:

> Sensations sweet,
> Felt in the blood, and felt along the heart . . .

Glen Cavaliero reminds me that John Cowper Powys, a century later, was a vitalist and a Nietzschean who loved to quote

Wordsworth. In *A Glastonbury Romance* and in *Weymouth Sands* Powys repeatedly emphasises his characters' pleasure in their own sensuous experience. And again one blinks, and has to remind oneself that the Powyses, like Wordsworth, were raised in the old Establishment culture of Christian Platonism, Oxbridge and the Church of England. How far they have moved!

Perhaps the best way to explain Wordsworth's extraordinary originality will be to recall the Platonic doctrine of the soul's pre-existence in the heavenly world. 'How like an angel came I down': in early infancy the child still remembers the heavenly world from which it has come and is thereby still able to see this world as Paradise. 'Heaven lies about us in our infancy'. Later, after the 'shades of the prison-house' have closed in, the poet keeps returning to his memories of childhood in order to recapture that first simple, innocent pleasure in life and sense-experience. According to the 'Immortality' ode, habit and custom are 'Hard as frost, and deep almost as life', which must be the first description of life as 'deep' in our literature. So in Wordsworth's poetry we may see a strain of incipient Nietzschean vitalism emerging from within the very heart of the old Christian Platonism – rather a wonderful thought. The heaven of religion is an alienated, mythicized representation of how we might be able to see *this* world, and of how we might be living *this* life.

To return to our main theme: during the second half of the twentieth century, many new idioms have come into common speech which reveal a strongly religious attitude to 'life', just *this* life. Many old ways of speaking about God and many religious attitudes have come to be refocused around a new object, 'life'. Exactly what 'life' is we will discuss later, but here are a few clues: it is clearly not quite the same as God, for it is finite, changing and processual. Like the Holy Spirit, though, it wells up, flows out, 'proceeds', or comes forth. It is pretty close to what in recent books I have called Being. Some people's use of the word is more biological and life-force-ish, and other people's is more social and cultural; but there is general agreement on the old Nietzschean maxim that one should above all find the courage to say Yes to life:

> Evil, what is evil?
> There is only one evil, to deny life . . .[11]

For a particularly vivid characterization by a great writer of the new religious sense of life, here are some passages from Virginia Woolf. The first shows life becoming almost personified, the second shows the sense in which it is always with us, and the third shows it as religiously fulfilling:

> The interest in life does not lie in what people do, nor even in their relations to each other, but largely in the power to communicate with a third party, antagonistic, enigmatic, yet perhaps persuadable, which one may call life itself.[12]

> Life is not a series of gig-lamps symmetrically arranged; life is a luminous halo, a semi-transparent envelope surrounding us from the beginning of consciousness to the end.[13]

> Life itself, every moment of it, every drop of it, here, this instant, now, in the sun, in Regent's Park, was enough.[14]

Taken together, these passages are so eloquent and striking as almost to provide the basic outline of a theology of life. *Where has all this come from?* I undertook to provide some genealogical stories, and here is the first.

In the English-speaking world, the chief progenitors of the new religious sense of life in common speech are (as we were told earlier) the lineage that runs Schopenhauer → Nietzsche → Lawrence → F. R. Leavis and then, through the many devoted and influential pupils of Leavis, fans out to schools and colleges across the English-speaking world in the period between the 1930s and the 1970s. Especially in his later writings, Leavis adopts Lawrence's use of religious language in connection with life, and makes 'life' almost a critical principle – notably when attacking 'the Eliotic despair of life'. Leavis's religious sense of life was at the cultural and social end of the spectrum: the critic does not judge literature from the standpoint of eternity, nor from the standpoint of biology, but from the standpoint of an actual human community with its own life, its own evolved meanings, its own valuations. The teacher of English, in Leavis's view, is a sort of parish clergyman, interpreting classic texts to a living community to which he owes a duty and of which he is himself also a member. We may or may not approve of this picture of the teacher of English as a preacher of literature; but at least it is clear that the Leavisite teacher affirms life, which means that he or she affirms and stands within a living tradition of humanly-evolved meanings and valuations – including, certainly, *spiritual* values. Leavis argues that Eliot's attempt to ground 'spiritual values' in an unknowable, timeless, transcendent realm is profoundly self-stultifying. Eliot is unhappy because he contradicts himself, using his own poetic life and creativity to deny life and human creativity in the name of a timeless Supremely Real which is wholly Other and therefore empty. No: for Leavis it is axiomatic that religion and spiritual values must be grounded in life; which means they must be grounded in the 'immemorial collaborative human creativity' that has given and still gives to us everything we live by.[15] The point here will bear repetition: Leavis argues that spiritual values – in the importance of which he passionately believes – *cannot* be grounded in God, and *must* be grounded in life.

That is the single most notable lineage that has parented our new religious sense of life; but there are several offshoots and affines as well. Wordsworth's influence was pervasive in the whole Victorian period. In addition, Schopenhauer's influence spread very widely during the later nineteenth century. Some of those influenced by him, like Turgenev and Proust, retained his pessimistic outlook; but others turned his doctrine of the Will in the direction of vitalism, so that the 'life-force' or the will-to-live might serve as some sort of replacement for the lost belief in a guiding and supporting Providence. The Will in us, associated particularly with the sex drive, is a power within us and a little distinct from us, with which we need to be in tune. In Britain, Thomas Hardy read and annotated Schopenhauer from the mid-1880s, and Hardy in turn was himself an influence upon Lawrence again, upon Conrad, and also upon such later vitalists as Dylan Thomas[16] and, in our own time, Ted Hughes.

What of Virginia Woolf's remarkable sense of life? It is worth remembering that, whatever one's doubts about turning Schopenhauer's doctrine of the Will into the basis for a vitalistic philosophy of life, Schopenhauer was in any case an evolutionist, and the first Western thinker to turn psychology in a biological direction. In the project of developing a fully biological understanding of the human self, Schopenhauer's key successors were of course Darwin and William James. Couple those three with the fact that Virginia Woolf was one of those who see and love life and good health very intensely because their own personal hold upon them is fragile, and one can begin to understand why she writes as she does.

In this first story about the origins of our new sense of life, we have referred to a number of creative thinkers and writers of the period around 1820–1960 in whose work the modern sense of self, the modern placing of the human being *in life* and in the living world, and modern biology-based psychology is taking shape. The thinking of most ordinary people until not very long ago was dominated by work, and by religious doctrine and strict moralism, or by political ideology. Only with the sudden great surge of prosperity since the Second World War have the mass of ordinary people gained the leisure time (and the access) for culture, for the development of subjectivity, and for straight-forward **enjoyment of life**. A consequence of the change is that instead of seeing life as a matter of obeying orders, people begin to think in terms of choosing one's own personal **lifestyle**. Rule-morality is replaced by the new expressionist morality of 'coming out' and being oneself. Ordinary people begin to want to do their own thing in their own way. It has become increasingly possible to democratize a kind of religious feeling for life, just *this* life, that a century ago was confined to a small circle of intellectuals.

This democratization has already changed working-class culture. Life has become a religious vocation. We say to the young: **You've got your life all before you** (*scil.*, you lucky devil). **It's up to you to make something of it. Don't waste your life!** Life is now a precious gift, an opportunity, a responsibility and a task. In that context we now feel sad when we hear an old person say, 'I've worked hard all my life', as if to say: 'At the end of our lives, people like me cannot expect to have any more to show for our lives than the fact that we worked hard and uncomplainingly and have endured this far. Now we deserve recompense in the form of life after death, or better pensions'. We feel sad when we hear all this, because it has already become anachronistic. People shouldn't still be trapped in the old view of this life as **a mere existence**, nothing but hard labour from beginning to end, and endured in the hope of a better life here-after. No: people's expectations ought now to be higher than that. They ought **to be getting more out of life** than that.

Why? How? How is it that we are coming to feel that just the living of this present life is a grand religious opportunity, responsibility and task? The genealogical story we've told so far has been a story about industrialization, rising prosperity, and a sudden huge amelioration of the conditions of life, first for the middle classes and then increasingly since the 1950s for the bulk of the old 'working' classes; and this, coupled with a general overspill of religious language away from its old specifically-religious site and into all the new spheres of life, **lifestyles** and **good things of life** that have been opened up to us. But we need a deeper account of why just life itself, just being **in the land of the living** has become something so intensely felt, so holy, so precious, so much a vocation and something to be cosmically grateful for.

We referred to F. R. Leavis's use of life itself as a critical principle, to be used to demolish T. S. Eliot. And we noted that Leavis's use of the word life is predominantly social and cultural. He sees literature and criticism as always grounded in, and always checked back against, the life of actual human communities. All language, all meanings, and all values are products of human creativity, conserved and accumulated with-in human cultural traditions. The poet always depends upon such a background, and ought not to try to write against it. It is self-defeating to use one's own creative powers to deny human creativity.

Taking Leavis's argument a stage further, one friend suggests to me that Leavis's use of 'life' as a critical touchstone may be seen as continuing the old English tradition that affects a preference for hard facts and **real life**. The story goes that after the Reformation religious interest in Britain switched to 'Nature', which meant land, livestock, horses, gardens, landscape, home and family, and attention to human diversity. We liked writing and art to be 'true to life'. It is on such grounds that John Dryden, in his essay *Of Dramatick Poesie* (1684) criticizes the French and praises Chaucer:

> Homer describ'd his heroes men of great appetites, lovers of beef broil upon the coals, and good fellows; contrary to the practice of the French Romances, whose heroes neither eat, nor drink, nor sleep, for love.[17]

And Dryden admires Chaucer's 'comprehensive Nature',

> because, as it has been truly observ'd of him, he has taken into the Compass of his *Canterbury Tales* the various Manners and Humours . . . of the whole English Nation, in his age . . . Even the ribaldry of the low characters is different: the Reeve, the Miller, and the Cook, are several Men, and distinguished from each other, as much as the mincing Lady Prioress, and the broad-speaking gap-toothed Wife of Bathe.[18]

Dryden's conclusion is that nothing changes very much. Chaucer's characters

> are still remaining in mankind, and even in England, though they are called by other names than those of Moncks, and Fryars, and Chanons and Lady Abbesses, and Nuns: for mankind is ever the same, and nothing is lost out of Nature, though everything is alter'd.[19]

In the next century, Samuel Johnson similarly praises

Shakespeare for his faithfulness to nature and to life, but again puts the main emphasis upon generalities:

> Shakespeare is above all writers, at least above all modern writers, the poet of nature; the poet that holds up to his readers a faithful mirror of manners and of life . . . His persons act and speak by the influence of those general passions and principles by which all minds are agitated, and the whole system of life is continued in motion . . . Shakespeare excels in accommodating his sentiments to real life . . .[20]

These classical texts, however, do not quite confirm my friend's hypothesis. When Johnson, Dryden and a whole line of others appeal to Nature, to real life, and to the ideal of being true to life, they are not using life as a critical touchstone in Leavis's sense, and they do not have anything approaching the intensely-religious attitude to life that we found in Virginia Woolf and in D. H. Lawrence. For Dryden and Johnson, 'life' is human actuality; it is motion indeed, but motion only within and relative to a much larger fixed and defining moral and natural framework. Human nature, the range of human types, and the broad comedy of English life remain the same for ever. In England everyone plays a character part, and it has been customary for people to be portrayed as being totally unaware of having become the comic characters that (to others) they all are. Hence the pervasive presence of irony throughout English life and utterance.

So where has the modern and highly-conscious *religious* sense of life come from? Our second genealogical story suggests that it is the long-term consequence of linguistic, and specifically *religious*, changes that took place at the Reformation. Before the Reformation, Christianity in the West was dominated by a very sharp distinction between the sacred and secular spheres, and between life in religion and life in the world. To a much greater extent than ever subsequently, Church and lay society were two distinct worlds, each with its own law-code, system of government, language and way of life. The religious life was very far from being ordinary biological or social life: it was celibate, under rule, and within the jurisdiction of the Church. A religious vocation was a call *into* religion; that is, it was a call out of the world and into the sacred realm, out of the vernacular language and into Latin, out of history and into the liturgical calendar.

Against this background, the Reformation was a violent revolt against the received form of sacred/secular distinction, a revolt whose full implications are even yet not fully worked out.[21] From the first, Luther wanted to teach the possibility of a holy life in the world, and the sanctity (or at any rate, the sanctifiability) therefore of marriage, of private, domestic and family life, of the vernacular language, and of a vocation to a purely secular calling. But Luther himself was of course not fully consistent on all these points. Marriage, for example, was not widely idealized or sanctified until the early nineteenth century, and not fully equalized as a relationship until the late twentieth century – by which time, alas, it was beginning to die out. It seems that our discovery of marriage came too late. The stock English idioms about **the sanctity of private life** and **the sanctity of the home,** or **of domestic life,** are of late-nineteenth-century origin. Sex is still not yet fully sanctified, despite Lawrence's best (and somewhat risible) efforts on its behalf – and perhaps never will be, for a reason allegedly given by Luther himself in his table-talk.[22] As for employments, we are still able to regard only some as vocations: the rest are just jobs.

Nevertheless, and even after these qualifications, the Reformation did open the way to a world in which the sacred and the profane spheres are no longer kept carefully separated, but instead increasingly coincide, with the long-term result that just 'life' – ordinary biological life, social life, communicative life – can eventually come to be experienced as being religious.

The result has often been a reversal of traditional valuations. In the Middle Ages, as in the Old Testament, childbirth created a state of ritual pollution. Women had to attend church to make the accustomed offerings and be purified. A form of this ritual of 'churching' survived the Reformation, and in Northern

England lingered on at least until the 1960s, even overlapping with the new epoch in which fathers began to attend the birth of their own children and to describe it as an awesome and religiously-uplifting experience, and not 'polluting' at all.

I mention *communicative* life, because in this revolution in values the adoption of the vulgar tongue, the vernacular language, for the scriptures, preaching and common prayer has in the long run had an enormously powerful democratizing and demystifying influence.[23] When Scripture is available in the vulgar tongue, it becomes possible to compare it with other books; when preachers use the vulgar tongue, we can compare their efforts with other forms of critical, interpretative and hortatory speech; and when public worship uses the vernacular we are invited to compare its language with the language we use on other formal occasions. During the 1960s, new vernacular versions of the Bible and the liturgy were produced, not only by protestant churches but even by the Roman Catholic Church, giving a very great fresh impetus to the process of secularization. The sacred ceases to be hidden, obscure, dark, fenced-off and highly concentrated. Instead it is *made plain*, and spreads around – which is a very good thing.[24]

Very well: the Reformation, by violently disrupting the established distinction between the sacred and secular realms, tended to blur them together in a way that gradually made it possible for people to experience, successively, domestic life, private life, working life, and finally just life itself as religious states.

The continuity is sometimes very striking, especially in art. Consider, for example, the way in which the art of the Low Countries recycles the old subject of the *Annunciation* as the *Woman Reading*. In the work of such an artist as Jan Vermeer the light still as in the past comes down from top left to fall upon a young woman alone in a room, but now it is natural and not supernatural light, and instead of the divine Word piercing directly into her body, the light falls upon the human words of a book or a letter in her hands. The Annunciation has been secularized, but the result still has the same calm, rapt and religious quality about it. Even today, painters still like *Woman Reading* as a subject, and it is still religious.

To take another and very different example, there are many large English country houses which before the Reformation were houses of religion. At the Reformation the old monastic estates were taken over, and the great buildings were converted to the use of the new landowners. But there were continuities. The entire household still gathered in the chapel for morning and evening prayers, and there were similarities in the social role, the organisation and the daily routine of the house under the old order and in the new. Architecturally, there is in some places visible continuity between the last grand lodgings built in early Tudor times for Priors and the houses built in later Tudor times for landowners. And for that matter, the older Oxford and Cambridge Colleges can look and be surprisingly like religious houses to this day. So can the Inns of Court in London, and many of the Public Schools.

The development has been slow. The old view that Nature is fallen, that Man is fallen, and that the whole of human existence under the present dispensation is unsatisfactory and in need of redemption remained strong. The sort of unhistorical realism that sees human life as held within a fixed and historically-unchanging framework remained strong, as we saw in commenting on Dryden and Johnson. The upshot was that only after Hegel and Darwin, only *after* the cultural revolution of the nineteenth century, were the conditions right for a fully-developed and autonomous religiousness of Life to appear.

When we have tasted it, we next want to ask ourselves: 'How did our ordinary everyday life-experience get to be and to remain so hideously debased and secularized for so long?'

An answer to this question will require, in our third genealogical story, a much deeper dig down into history. We begin from the old and very important distinction between mortals and immortals.

The Immortals are figures such as gods and the most-nearly-divine kings. They are immortal because their function is to maintain the continuity of life, and especially the continuity of the state. They embody values, authority, and the state's insatiable self-feeding will to ever-wider sway.[25] The gods never sleep and never die; their reign is uninterrupted. That God is a *living* god is one of his most prominent attributes. The gods are always seen as having the very highest degree of life – which means alertness, creative energy, vitalizing power, and will to rule.

As for kings, it was customary to acclaim them by wishing them long life. May the King live for ever! God save the King! Long to reign over us. Grant him in health and wealth long to live. *Vivat*. The importance of the King's apparent good-health to public morale was so great that within living memory a somewhat-sickly British monarch was rouged before his public appearances. The death of a king was the saddest and most ill-omened event, and various rituals sought to mitigate its fearsomeness. Conventionally there was no interregnum: the Heir-apparent succeeds automatically upon the instant of the old king's death. The King is dead; long live the King! As for the dead King, he does not cease to be a king and does not cease to reign. He is very commonly enthroned amongst the dead in a Hall of the Kings, and perhaps also in the Underworld with Osiris. From his new underground place of permanent enthronement he continues to endorse and validate the reign of his successor. Thus language and ritual everywhere used to go as far as possible towards making the king an Immortal. The king *is* his kingship, and his *kingship* at least is immortal. From Japan to Peru he was commonly described as a Son of God and a child of heaven, assimilated as far as a human being can be to the everlasting life of the gods; and the object of all this was to do everything possible to secure the uninterrupted power and authority of the state.

Throughout the entire period of agricultural civilization – up to five or six thousand years – there was a close relationship between theology, politics and royal ideology. It had a massive effect upon the idea of life. The price that had to be paid for the creation of the state and the security it promised was that ordinary human beings had to suffer relative devitalization and disempowerment, and learn to live vicariously – that is, through their relation to someone greater than themselves, whom they served. When life has been equated with pure creative, vitalizing and legislative power's unlimited self-affirmation and sovereignty, it becomes clear that life properly belongs *only* to the immortals – the gods and the king. Life is theirs for ever: death will be ours, soon. Meanwhile, we serve them. Perhaps if we are fortunate they may graciously choose to reward us for faithful service by co-opting us into their company and into some measure of participation in their deathless life – if our names turn out to be written in the Book of Life, that is.

In this world-view we human beings are not truly alive naturally and in our own right. By nature, we are mere mortals under sentence of death; and this merely natural biological life of ours is as such insignificant. What we must aspire after is adoption into or participation in the larger, the supernatural, the *eternal* life of the heavenly world and the Immortals. The state, thought of as divinely instituted and bodied forth in the person of the king, links the two worlds, and in the service of the king one already participates in a larger life than one's own.

We now see that for several millennia, Life was split in the same way as was Being.[26] That is, Being was split between Eternal Being (to which was ascribed all the value) and mere temporal 'Becoming', the ordinary person's experience: and in the same away, Life was split between the Life Everlasting enjoyed by the Immortals in the heavenly world (and to which was ascribed all the value), and the mere temporal existence of a mortal gravitating towards death, which was the ordinary person's fate.

It becomes clear that there waits to be written a history of the forgetting of Life, parallel to Heidegger's history of the forgetting of Being. The power of Being and the capacity to live responsively in Being were hived off, stripped out of the world ordinary human life and experience, and projected out into a timeless and curiously sterile noumenal world of absolute Being, leaving humans floundering confusedly in the empty flux of Becoming. And, in a similar way, at about the time of the coming of the gods and the first development of the State, the power of Life, its self-renewing creative energy and joy, was stripped out of the world of ordinary human life and concentrated in the world of the Immortals, and perhaps also upon the State and divine kingship. It came to motivate their drive to unlimited power and sovereignty. Ordinary human life became as people say, **a mere existence**, hastening towards death, which could regain worth only by being devoted instrumentally to the service of a god or a king. To be meaningful, a human existence must be lived 'in service'; and to this day when ordinary people pose the question about **the Meaning of Life** they are expressing the wish to hear a story about a great Lord's personal plan, for them to serve him. They want to hear how by entering his service they can gain a sense of 'meaning' for themselves, and pick up for themselves a few sparks of his own superabundant vital energy. This will make them **feel more alive.** And so they continue to assume what has been assumed for thousands of years: that a human being can enjoy Life only vicariously. We were not born free; we were born to serve. So for about 5000 years, an assumption that a state of alienation from Life is normal has shaped religion, morality, and culture generally. Indeed, to this day, vicarious participation in lives better and greater than our own is a very large part of everyday cultural activity for many or most human beings. For them soap opera is religious drama, because they still equate religiousness with secondhand living. People may say: **I want to live my own life**, but as yet only a few really mean it. Most still see themselves as believers, fans and spectators, fit only for vicarious life. Pessimism about our life remains religious orthodoxy, and is widely saluted as such when people meet it in T. S. Eliot's *Four Quartets*:

> . . . that which is only living
> Can only die.[27]

One sees why Leavis was so nettled by such a dismal line: for Eliot, our life as such is without value, because it is merely mortal.

When did the alienation of Life from human beings and the consequent forgetting of Life begin? The conventional Nietzschean answer would presumably go: between Homer and Plato, or indeed between Heraclitus and Plato. Now I'd say: much earlier. Even Gilgamesh is already in big trouble, as is shown by his fear of death. This is ironical, because Gilgamesh is *himself* a king! Evidently he is not taken in by his own royal ideology, which declared him to be a demigod, the son of a king and a goddess. What brings him down is his love for Enkidu, a lesser mortal. So the forgetting of Life began when human beings started to see themselves as mere mortals doomed to die, in comparison with One supremely great and Immortal, whose superabundant power of life gave him (or It) the right to absolute rule over them. When people first began to think this way – perhaps in about 3500 BCE at Uruk/Warka? – Life had already been drained away from them and had become Another's property, something they could hope to enjoy only at one remove, vicariously or by Grace.

When did human beings begin to remember their own direct religious relation to Life? Here the case is very different from that of Being, because the remembering of life has already largely (or at any rate, partially) happened. It begins with a growing interest in the only-human experience of the human subject, and in the drama of human relationships. It is apparent in the rise of the novel to become the dominant literary form, and in the rise of modern biology and psychology since Darwin and William James. With Nietzsche and Bergson[28] philosophy seeks to return into time and into life, and one might say that phenomenology (Husserl, Merleau-Ponty) was philosophy's most systematic attempt to remember Life, and that existentialism was philosophy's most energetic attempt actually to appropriate Life and to *live* it. Since existentialism, there has alas been a minor recession, but surely it will be only temporary.

One sign of the change in our view of life is to ask ourselves: where do we look for a background against which to set ourselves, see ourselves, understand ourselves? To borrow a phrase, what's our significant Other? The answer used to be couched in terms of tradition, Scripture and the supernatural world. Now, it's Life: and to help us to see our life a bit better we often look to the animal world from which we have emerged.

In religious thought, no subsequent writer of our relation to life has yet surpassed or even equalled Kierkegaard, and especially his discourses on texts from the Sermon on the Mount. His strongest rival is Miguel de Unamuno, author of *The Tragic Sense of Life*, 1913 – but it must be said that neither of them, nor any other philosopher, has yet wrestled with our human biology, our bodiliness, our bodily sensations, and our experience of our own physiology. We are not spirits, floating in life; we *are* our life, our lives, our bodies. In the novel nobody, so far as I know, has yet bettered or even equalled D. H. Lawrence and Virginia Woolf – two characters very much at odds with each other. Evidently the Religion of Life resembles the Religion of Being, of which it is a variant: both need to be written, but both are difficult. Nevertheless, they *need* to be written, if we humans are to recover ourselves.

The last genealogical question we need to raise is this: was there ever an Eden, an Age of Gold when humans were in the right relationship to the time of their own lives, and so were able to live magnificently and forget death? I answer No, and will explain.

3

Ways of Relating Oneself to Life

There never was a prehistory in which human beings lived in the right religious relationship to life, and I'll tell you why. The new religiousness *of life* that has been developing in the last 150 years or so is not quite autonomous and not heteronomous; it is, one might say, *bionomous*.[1] It represents not a return to simple pre-historical – and perhaps pre-reflective – animal immediacy, but rather a postmodern, highly conscious, elective or *chosen* immediacy. It is slightly humorous, in that we simultaneously semi-personify life and mock ourselves for doing so. **How's life treating you? Is life good to you? Oh! life's a bitch!** – But life is not a substance, a distinct being. It is, metaphorically at least, more like a milieu within which we live, or a continuously-flowing current that upholds us, propels us, flows through us, and when differentiated by language just is *us*, our own selves. It is so close to me that it is both me and not-me. It is what vitalizes me, and is released afresh in me by what-ever **makes me feel most alive.** Hence the tendency, manifest in the popular idioms, to talk about life as we talk about luck or fortune, in a tone of mock-exasperation which (as in the case of marriage) is entirely compatible with deep moral commitment.[2]

As I say, this complicated, ironical, passionate, *bionomous* religiousness is new, so new that one might very reasonably call it late-Modern or postmodern. It begins to appear as far back as Kierkegaard, with his concern for the way we relate ourselves to what he calls 'existence', and his account of the self as a process of becoming. But it would be absurdly anachronistic to suppose that people thought like this in prehistoric times. Obviously they didn't.

Animal Immediacy

The earliest and simplest sort of relation to life that we need discuss is animal immediacy, classically typified in the Sermon on the Mount by the birds of the air, and in Virginia Woolf by a moth that she watches fluttering against the window-pane.[3] After an opening paragraph describing the landscape outside she pulls back to look at the moth:

> The same energy which inspired the rooks, the ploughmen, the horses, and even, it seemed, the lean barebacked downs, sent the moth fluttering from side to side of his square of the window-pane. One could not help watching him. One was indeed, conscious of a queer feeling of pity for him. The possibilities of pleasure seemed that morning so enormous and so various that to have only a moth's part in life, and a day moth's at that, appeared a hard fate, and his zest in enjoying his meagre opportunities to the full, pathetic.[4]

I am annoyed that she doesn't say what species it is, and probably doesn't really know for sure even whether it's male or female. She lacks our awareness of what a highly evolved creature a moth is, and how acute are its senses. Since small flying creatures are usually phototropic – that is, they fly towards the light – window glass is utterly lethal to them, but they have had no time to adapt to it. It isn't fair to portray the unfortunate moth as a dim creature, but I fear that Mrs Woolf is *looking down* upon it as some kind of social inferior. I'd have persuaded it towards the open window and out into the open air by now. Lawrence Sterne's uncle Toby did that for a mere fly, fully two centuries earlier.

However, the moth gradually wins a certain respect from its observer as it battles on undaunted:

> What he could do he did. Watching him, it seemed as if a fibre, very thin but pure, of the enormous energy of the world had been thrust into his frail and diminutive body. As often as he crossed the pane, I could fancy that a thread of vital light became visible. He was little or nothing but life.

Yet, because he was so small and so simple a form of the energy that was rolling in at the open window and driving its way through so many narrow and intricate corridors in my own brain and in those of other human beings, there was something marvellous as well as pathetic about him. It was as if someone had taken a tiny bead of pure life and decking it as lightly as possible with down and feathers, had set it dancing to show us the true nature of life.[5]

In a while the moth settles, exhausted and (no doubt) dehydrated. She watches it die. Now the moth

. . . lay most decently and uncomplainingly composed. Oh yes, he seemed to say, death is stronger than I am.[6]

There is something theological about Virginia Woolf's vitalism in this passage – as indeed there was also in the vitalism of many of her contemporaries. As God is thought to be both everywhere and wholly present at every point, so the rolling energies of the world are both ubiquitous and also brought to a specially-intense point-focus in living things such as the moth and also his observer's highly-active, troubled brain. One stuff rolling everywhere makes and unmakes us all.

There is also a touch of the reflective observer's reluctant and even slightly envious admiration for the animal's unreflective, immediate relation to life. It is life, it is its own life. It doesn't stop to think; it just does what a moth has to do. There is a simple uncomplicated dignity in the way it loves life, battles to the end, and then dies without complaint. Do we, can we ever hope to do any better than that? A contemporary of Virginia Woolf, G. K. Chesterton, somewhere remarks that nobody ever felt it necessary to slap a crocodile on the back and tell it to cheer up and 'Be a crocodile!'. A man very often has a big problem about how to be a man, but no crocodile ever found any difficulty in being a crocodile. Crocodiles simply do not have problems. They don't need to be told to 'Be yourself!' or to 'Become what you are'. Why? Because they don't think. They have no anxieties, very few memories and no worries about the future. They just live in the present, without language, simply coinciding with themselves in the moment and in immediate relation to life. Unreflectively and unhesitatingly, they just act out their own natures, and do what crocodiles have to do.

Is that what we were once like, and is that the condition we should hope to regain? Many people think so. They tend to map modern evolutionary biology onto the old Western theology of original righteousness, the Fall and the long drama of redemption, with the result that they tend to associate their ideas about humankind's lost happiness with their ideas about Nature, gardens, animals, childhood and the general unhealthiness of thinking. Did not most of my older readers have parents who considered that it was 'morbid' to have one's nose in a book all the time, and used to tell them to get out into the fresh air and exercise themselves in some way that also involved animals? Being themselves small animals, and therefore fortunate in being closer to Eden than adults, children – so parents used to think – should live in or close to the blessed primal condition of animal immediacy for as long as they can. As for adults, the nearest we can get to an immediate relation to our own biological life is perhaps by immersing ourselves in the twentieth century's biggest quasi-religion – sport. When we watch a trained performer such as an ice-skater we are thrilled by an impression of superb effortlessness. It seems to symbolize the possibility of life without hesitation or thought; just getting everything right straight off, as an animal does.

But I don't agree with any of this. Even animals live much more in the world of signs than has traditionally been supposed. Behaviours initiated by the animal very commonly – perhaps almost always – have some general significance, and animal response is perhaps always response to the *general* significance of the stimulus. Indeed, the whole study of animal behaviour, which has grown so fast and has had such great success since the 1930s, has rested upon the presumption that animal behaviours can be *interpreted* – i.e., that they *do* have general significance. But generality involves reference to other occasions, past or future, actual or possible, that involve or involved the presentation of the same sign. So, if any bit of animal behaviour has been acquired and has general significance, then that animal does *not* live in a relation to life of pure immediacy. And indeed, learning has in fact been demonstrated even amongst some invertebrates.

As for us human beings, our relation to life is always mediated by reflection. We are always in language, always awake to symbolic meaning, and therefore always in some degree 'conscious'. In this sense at least, Descartes' doctrine that 'the soul always thinks' and never 'sleeps' is correct. And it is precisely because our relation to life is always to some extent mediated – whether by generality, or by the sign, or by 'thought' – that it is possible for us to have a religious attitude to life.

The Anxiety of Reflection

Reflection, I am saying, is always present in human beings. We do not simply coincide with our life. We stand back just a little, opening a gap for reflection, deliberation, consideration, hesitation – in a word, consciousness. And the slight difference between us and life opens a religious relationship, as Moses recognizes when he commands Israel: 'Therefore choose life, that you may live'. Today's idiom says: **Why don't you switch off the TV and get a life!**, which amounts to much the same thing – except that Moses continues by explaining that the way to choose life is by loving God, 'for he is thy life, and the length of thy days'.[7]

You may well wonder why two-and-a-half millennia ago the imperative 'Choose life' had the same force as the imperative 'Choose God'; whereas today's life-centredness has become post-theistic. That is odd, but it is a question that we must defer for the present. Our present concern is that the question of choosing or refusing life arises only for beings who have become a little distanced from life by reflection.

I am saying that wherever there is language, wherever there is a universal term, wherever there is a sign, there is a measure at least of reflection or consciousness. The organism is not wholly immersed in its own present experience. Indeed, language can never fix just upon simple animal immediacy. All meaning is a bit sideways, so that linguistic meaning always arrives a little belatedly, anticipates what may yet be to come, alludes to other states of affairs that may obtain elsewhere, and hints at other possible constructions even of what is presently given. Do you have a spouse who, if you say something seemingly innocent like, 'Let's go for a walk', immediately thinks of at least a dozen things that you might be getting at by saying that? Don't laugh at Spouse. Spouse is perfectly correct. Language is like that, always. It conjures up innumerable possibilities: it creates thought and suspicions. So a language-using being is a thinking being, a being that is always reviewing dozens of hypotheses at high speed and therefore is not purely and immediately engaged in its own life. A language-using being is one who is always surrounded by a swarm of possibilities. The English may equate innocence with mindless immediacy, but no language-using being can be innocent in that sense.

But if human beings are fated to reflection, then by the same token they are always threatened by anxiety, by the wish that the past had been different and by the uncertainties of the future.[8] Anxiety has a very strong propensity to become a trap, for the very reflectiveness that enables Virginia Woolf to look thoughtfully at the moth, to pity the futility of the moth's struggles, and even a little to admire the moth's commitment to life for as long as life lasts, *also* makes it quite impossible that she herself could ever become like the moth. Reflection is a one-way ticket; you can only get *more* reflective, you can't ever go back. The intellectual's nostalgia for the lost happiness of some earlier and simpler form of consciousness is a dead end, a trap.

Suppose that as a result of an historical catastrophe human beings, over a period of four or five generations, *were* to be forced back. Suppose that they were to revert from being highly-conscious, even ironized, postmodern city-dwellers to being Dark-Age peasants wholly enclosed within a sacred cosmology. (It has happened before: maybe it will happen again. Who knows?) Then: Would the peasants be better off? No –

because they would have utterly lost the point of view from which they could judge themselves to have become better off.

The point here is one that Hegel understood. Forget the silly idea that history just *happens* to be written by the victors. The truth is that only the victors *can* write history. History can only be written as a story of the progressive widening of human horizons, as each age's world-view and form of consciousness is understood and taken up into the more inclusive understanding of its successor. The historian who is within the process can reconstruct its earlier stages. But suppose that the historical sequence has run in the opposite direction. Could one write *from within the process* an historical narrative of the progressive *loss* of social structure, *loss* of knowledge, *loss* of technologies and narrowing of horizons? No, because *this* loss entails losing the knowledge of what it is that has been lost. How could you write a book in such a way that, by the time you get to the end of the book, you can no longer understand your own earlier chapters?

So reflection is a one-way street. It can't go back; it can only become more so. It leads unstoppably to our postmodern condition, in which we have seen through everything, and fear that we have become terminally-ironized, morally impotent spectators of life. We know it all, and therefore can do nothing. All we are fit for is looking at screens. Our helplessness causes us to feel self-contempt: hence the coarse violence of that late-Nineties phrase, **Get a life!** Why don't we **start living?**

Living by Dogmatic Faith

By an almost-Hegelian logic, language-using beings become gradually more and more reflective – and therefore more threatened by anxiety. As one's horizons expand, they encompass a wider and wider range of alternative vocabularies, interpretations, constructions of the world. One is surrounded by an ever-increasing swarm of ghostly possibilities that may or may not materialize. As Kierkegaard remarks, the anxious person is afraid, afraid of nothing,[9] because the object of his anxiety is merely the possible; it is freedom, it is life's pure contingency. There is 'really' no thing out there to fear. But this observation does not solve the problem of anxiety, as we see when we recall that what most of all is a mere 'nothing' is also the 'object' of our most intense anxiety, namely death. The anxiety is utterly irrational: the thought that my life did not happen to be set in the nineteenth century causes me no anxiety, so why should I be troubled by the thought that by 2015 or so the world will be getting on fine without me? And if I am quite easy about giving up my consciousness to sleep, why should I not be just as easy about giving it up to death?

So death is nothing, truly nothing – but still it causes anxiety so great as to spill over and affect all our life too. For is not life itself everywhere utterly contingent, trembling, determined, fragile, agitated, threatened? And are not all our values and beliefs – even the most cherished of them – similarly contingent? Thus anxiety, having consumed all else, next consumes the self as well:

> All existence makes me anxious, from the smallest fly to the mysteries of the Incarnation; the whole thing is inexplicable to me, I myself most of all; to me all existence is infected, I myself most of all.[10]

This all-consuming anxiety goes back a long way. There are eloquent reports of it in the Bible,[11] and even more in Hellenistic antiquity. One might trace it back as far as Sumer, which was the most anxious of the early civilizations. It is hard to see how someone caught up in it can escape, except by faith that somehow, somewhere, Someone or something has got that huge swarm of finite possibilities under firm control. *Any* doctrine that tells us that the future course of events is predetermined is a huge relief, whether it be astrology, or mechanistic determinism, or orthodox predestinarian theism. If I can be assured that there is but one scenario for the future, then I can study it and adapt myself to it. I know where I am. I can act, I can **start living**.

In addition, however, we need to be reassured that there is a kind of life that is not itself debilitated by trembling, unstable nerve-racking contingency; a kind of life that will stabilize us subjectively; a kind of life not threatened by time or chance, and in which we can participate. In a word, what the axial religions call salvation, release, eternal life. Faith is a way of living in anticipation of eternal life in a future world where there will be no contingencies and no unfulfilled possibilities. Faith writes off this world and this life and instead lives on the basis of dogmatic promises and a foretaste or foreshadowing of a Real Life that is yet to come.

For a very long period – and at least from −500 to +1500 CE – it seemed to the majority of the most reflective people that the only way to escape from all-consuming, disabling anxiety, guilt, and despair was by believing in and identifying with Something almighty and everliving, something supremely Alive and in control of life, that left nothing to chance and promised absolute security. But a price had to be paid: one must commit oneself to serve a communal dream of absolute power and control; one must demote one's own merely-human, living-creature's perspective upon the world; and one must write off everything to do with the senses, the passions, the body and mundane biological life. If you can learn to accept that you can never fully *live* your ordinary life, you will become able, and perhaps even find yourself *impelled*, to believe in the possibility of a post-mortem super-life.

Gradually, gradually, between the high Middle Ages and the nineteenth century, the price to be paid for this dream of life at last, not here but hereafter, came to seem too high, and the relative valuations of things implicit in it came to appear wrong and insupportable. The intellectual and spiritual journey involved between the world after Anselm, the twelfth century, and the world after Nietzsche, the twentieth and later centuries, is the greatest spiritual odyssey in human history. It is the great return to life. It is completed when we are happy to say that we would prefer to have *this* life, biological life in the here and now, rather than the old sort of eternal life; and that we prefer to be ordinary mortals rather than immortals. The angel in Wim

Wenders' film *Wings of Desire* – recently remade as *City of Angels* – has to choose between an immortal but passionless life, and an earthly mortal life in which love is possible. We know which he chose, and we know which we would choose: love outweighs death. And when at last we find the courage to choose life, this mortal life, we come back to life and to a new, voluntary and solar immediacy.

Solar Immediacy

More than anything else, it has been the Darwinian theory of biological evolution – together with its spin-off over the whole range of the human sciences – that has persuaded us to give up the fantasy of a trans-biological kind of life, and has persuaded us to come back into our own biology-based life.

Exactly what the word 'life' means has been deliberately deferred. For many young persons it seems to mean noisy social-izing on a large scale, and especially in city centres during the small hours of the morning. Very well; but that too is biology-based, just as much as is being a tree, or a feeling. So biology-based life is simply the sort of life you and I presently enjoy, chancy, time-bound, bodily and finite though it is. And by 'solar immediacy' in the present context I mean a way of overcoming anxiety by saying an all-out religious Yes to our life, as it is and without falsifying it. Nearly the whole history of religion has in one way or another represented an attempt to allay anxiety, and to stabilise the self and the world, by falsifying life and usually also by denying death. But my thesis in this book is that in very recent years many or most people have at last become able to say a religious Yes to biological life and to their own mortality. For example, as I write, the local Anglican diocese (Ely) has announced that it has begun to look for, and proposes to open, a woodland burial ground, quite openly responding to the growing popular view that when we die our remains are and should be recycled back into the environment. This clearly implies general acceptance nowadays that the old supernatural-ist view of human destiny is defunct, and the church appears ready to give that view (or to risk seeming to give that view) its tacit concurrence. Popular idioms have long suggested that we end simply as corpses, 'pushing up the daisies' – or, as the German idiom has it, 'looking up at the radishes from underneath' – and most people are now content to leave it at that.

Going over to a fully biology-based understanding of human existence means amongst other things giving up the idea of the self as a metaphysical substance, to be kept pure and undefiled during its journey through this world to its true home in the world beyond. Instead we learn to see the self as thoroughly interwoven with its environment, physical, social and cultural. It is adapting and changing all the time. It is not sharp-edged, stable and self-identical. Religion in the past very commonly attempted to define and maintain a clear boundary around the self; but it does not have clear boundaries. The self (I like being infuriatingly heretical) is more like an open *market*. It is constantly *trading* or exchanging, chemically, socially, linguistically. It is porous all over, its boundaries are shifting, and like the amoeba it changes shape. It takes in, it gives out, and like a candle it slowly burns down.

The self, in short, is a process in time – more like a role than a thing. It is a construct, a transient effect similar to the production of a character, a *dramatis persona*, by an actor during a theatrical performance. We make ourselves – or rather, we *project* our selves – by expressing ourselves as we go along. And when the play is over, the lights go out and the curtain falls.

People say: 'In my time', 'In my day', meaning 'When I was at that period of life when one is centre stage, a *jeune première*, in the limelight . . .' Thereafter one gradually becomes, first a character-part, then a spectator, and finally a memory.

So the self is a transient, biology-based, cultural product. Timebound, its course runs through a number of stages. And as we come to accept that this is how it is with us, we give up the idea that our life-task is to develop a fully-formed, perfected, immortalizable self for eternity, and instead we embrace the 'expressionist' and postmodern idea of our life as being like performance-art. We should be happy simply to 'come out' and play our part, strut our stuff, do our thing, make our contribution, and generally put on a good show. We should be as committed to the passing show of existence as Kirsten Flagstad was to each performance she gave.[12] That is solar immediacy – **to live as if one had a vocation to life**: to live 'Till death thy endless mercies seal / And make the sacrifice complete' (Wesley's hymns are sometimes remarkably prescient: not life *after* death, but life *unto* death). That is the new meaning we give to the ancient biblical imperative 'Choose life!' And we are cured of anxiety because we are no longer in any way trying to keep up a pretence that things are other than they are.

4

Bio-theology

How far do the new idioms about life and the new religious attitudes to life express a stateable and coherent new religious philosophy of life, or perhaps 'bio-theology'?

The answer, shortly, is: rather more than you might have expected. But there are two main restrictions. The first is that the idioms do not suppose life to be as morally consistent and perfect as God was thought to be. One cannot help being aware that there is **a dark side of life**, as well as **the sunny side of life**. Life is sometimes very sweet, sometimes capricious, sometimes a strict teacher, sometimes dark and mysterious, sometimes sublimely indifferent, and sometimes just implacably cruel. (It may however strike you that the God of the Hebrew Bible could seem equally volatile, varied and unpredictable.) And the second restriction is that two distinct traditions have influenced the emergent late-Modern or postmodern religiousness of life. Thomas Hardy and Sigmund Freud are more influenced by Greek epic and tragedy, with their powerful ideas of *moira*, fate and *ananke*, necessity, whereas D. H. Lawrence's language about life is usually drawn straight from the New Testament and from protestantism. What is most striking, however, is the discovery that even after due allowance has been made for these two points, the idioms still turn out to express a surprisingly coherent religious philosophy of life. I summarize it under fourteen heads, giving in each case, first a number, then a title which names the corresponding theme in the older orthodoxies, then a short 'credal' formulation, and finally a few illustrative modern idioms in **bold** type.

The reader will find it helpful to reflect on each idiom – and especially, as I have often said before, upon the prepositions. *In* life, and *of* life, for example. Think about the circumstances in which each idiom is used. In many cases one may also consider which idiom or biblical text did the same job in the older Christian orthodoxy. One can then ask whether the ordinary person was better equipped – that is, had access to better linguistic resources for coping with life —under the old order or in the new.

1. *Transcendence and Immanence, Otherness and Inwardness.* Life is a self-propagating and self-giving power and an encompassing milieu that is everywhere around us, and also is present in its whole reality and energy within each living thing. In being both all about us and also energetically present within us, life resembles the divine Spirit, and is therefore spoken of in the traditional imagery of fire and wind-or-breath. It stirs, moves, buzzes and hums.

> The first stirrings of life
> A start in life
> The gift of life
> The miracle of life
> A spark of life
> Signs of life
> The breath of life
> The kiss of life
> Full of life
> Life-force
> Put some life into it!
> I take my life in my hands
> For the life of me
> I'm getting on in life, now
> I've had my life

2. *Mystery.* Life is a mystery, a riddle, an enigma. Sometimes it can appear, like Fate, as a dark inscrutable Adversary of humankind. Sometimes it is a dance that we must join, or a seductress that entices us. At other times, life can seem wilful,

like a partner whose whims must be put up with good-humouredly.

> Is there an answer to life's riddle?
> The meaning of life
> The big questions of life
> The mystery of life
> Life's a lottery
> (with a shrug) That's life!
> That's what life is all about

3. *Realism.* Life is personified, but only semi-personified, and sometimes not even so much as that. Some idioms express a consciously non-realistic view of 'life'. The way *we* construct *it* makes it look to us the way it does.

> How's life been treating you lately?
> Life's been good to me
> He's had a hard life – but then, he's made life hard for himself
> Life is what you make it
> You only get out from life what you put into it
> I want to get back to living a normal life
> I want to live my own life
> I want my life back

4. *Holiness.* Life is the religious object – awesome, holy, sacred, demanding.

> The sanctity of life / holiness of life
> All life is sacred
> The miracle of new life
> 'Everything that lives is holy'[1]

5. *Vocation.* Life challenges us, sets us a task, demands commitment, and gives us only one chance.

> You've got your whole life before you
> You only live once/You only have one life

You have to face up to life's challenges
You can't run away from life
Today is the first day of the rest of your life
An aim in life
A mission in life
You need a purpose in life
A way of life / A path in life, life-path / Walks of life

6. *Faith and the Affirmation of Life.* Life above all else demands total commitment; indeed through commitment to life we get access to all other values. Life is almost the key to value. One must put life first, love life and say Yes to life. Conversely, someone who consistently sails under false colours and is untrue to life is said to be **living a lie** (cf. Ger. *Lebenslüge*). In life-talk faithfulness and truthfulness are in effect synonymous.

'A gentle faith in life itself'[2]
Trust life / Always look on the bright side of life
Commitment to life
True to life
Faithful to life / living a lie
Get a life!
A life worth living/not worth living
She loved life/was in love with life
The value of life
Quality of life
Life-loving, Life-enhancing

7. *Sin.* It is a grave sin **to despair of life, to hold life cheap,** or gratuitously to take innocent life. It is **a crime,** even **a blasphemy,** against life.

Pro life
The right to life
You've got entirely the wrong attitude to life
A sin against life

8. *Conversion*. Conversion to life is a radical change in one's attitude to life, through which one can get a new sense of purpose in life.

> You take life too much for granted
> You need to change your whole attitude to life
> You need an aim, a purpose in life
> My life isn't going anywhere
> Something to live for/to live by

9. *Providence*. There is a minimal moral order in this world, at least in the sense that if you say Yes to life you will live, but if you reject life, life will reject you. And life does have very important lessons to teach us: a French idiom says, *attends de connaître la vie pour juger*, wait until you know something about life before you pass judgment.

> Life goes on/must go on
> What life has in store for us
> What lessons life has to teach us
> I went to the university of life (Horatio Bottomley, 1920)
> Wherever our life may carry us/take us
> Life takes us hither and thither
> What life sends

10. *Acceptance, thanksgiving and resignation*. These classic religious attitudes are retained in non-objective form. One accepts it all, is grateful for everything, and says Amen to what must be. A counter-current, however, praises people who have 'fought to the last' against, for example, cancer. Because life is a *finite* religious object, it makes religious sense to fight *for* life against an enemy of life.

> Take life as it comes
> I feel grateful for life/to be alive
> Life's good!
> Such is life
> Fight for life/for one's own life/for someone else's life

11. *Joy in life*. Commitment to and faith in life brings religious joy in life. Some pursuits and occasions are especially precious because **they make us feel more alive**. Are such things sacraments of life?

> **This is the life!**
> **She's full of the joys of life**
> **Zest for life/lust for life/rage for life**
> **She's bubbly, life-loving**
> **I feel most alive when . . .** (compare German, *Lebensgefühl*)
> **I'm having the time of my life**

12. *Eschatology*. **Life is short**; it may end at any time. We should **make the most of life** while we have it.

> **Life is not a dress-rehearsal**
> **Live life to the full/a full life**
> **Live life one day at a time**
> **Where there's life there's hope** (ancient : *dum spiro spero*)
> **Life's short**
> **At my time of life I treat each new day as a bonus**
> **Take life as it comes**

13. *Tempting God*. Numbered 13, because it is anomalous and risky, is the path of tempting life rather as our forbears *tempted fate*, or *tempted God*. In a few exceptional people we may admire it; but one cannot encourage it. It 'courts' disaster.

> **Life caught up with him**
> 'Live dangerously' (Nietzsche)
> **Living on the edge**
> **Live hard**
> **Live fast, die young** (compare **Stay pretty, die young**)

14. *Being godless or bereft*. A person who is alienated from life, whether by some misfortune, or by inability to break out of the rut and choose life, is said to be *going through the motions*, stuck in *a mere existence*, or (with a shrug) *'surviving'*. (Compare Ephesians 2.12.)

Don't give up on life
I'm missing out on life
Life has passed me by

In this summary I have quoted some hundred or so idioms in **bold** type. We turn now to the *Shorter Oxford English Dictionary* of 1933, which continued to be reprinted with corrections until the 1970s. My edition of 1972 has a substantial entry s.v. 'life', but of the hundred or so idioms I have cited only *one*, **life-force**, appears in the Dictionary.

This is as one would expect. During the first third of the twentieth century orthodox Darwinism was on the defensive and there was a great deal of vitalism about, propagated by Henri Bergson and many English writers. The term 'life-force' was popular as a half-pagan synonym for God. That **life-force** should have reached the Dictionary is therefore not surprising. But it is notable that none of the other idioms makes it. Hence the hypothesis upon which I am resting a good deal of my argument in this book: the new way of thinking about life, and the large body of idioms associated with it that I am trying to demonstrate has become part of the ordinary person's wisdom of life only in the past thirty to fifty years. The Bible and orthodox monotheism have faded; and this seems to be what is coming in to replace them. Although it is a popular cliché that our society has become religiously very pluralistic, the body of idioms that we are examining suggests that on the contrary there is a strong emergent consensus.

Turning now to the full *OED* Second Edition of 1989, reprinted with corrections in 1991, we find a very large and detailed entry of some fifteen columns on 'life'. The number of my idioms that I find there reported now rises to about ten, by the addition of such items as **That's life, Life's like that, To live one's own life, Such is life, Life-enhancing** and **Life-lover**. Three beautiful phrases that I have so far missed are given: **come to life** (compare *come into being*), **to see life** (compare *to see the world*), and the archaic vocative use of **my life** to mean *my Dearest*. But the new meaning of 'life' and the new religious sense of life that is our topic remains unmentioned and is barely hinted at. Two or three citations show it coming. There is one good one from Lawrence: 'We are really far more life-stupid than the dead Greeks' (from *Fantasia of the Unconscious*, vii.15), and there are citations in connection with the term **life-world** which introduce the names of Edmund Husserl and Maurice Merleau-Ponty. This is important, because, if I am right, the new religious centrality of life is connected with the theme, very widespread in twentieth-century philosophy, of the philosophical priority of ordinary life and ordinary language. When belief in the *philosophical* priority of ordinary life has struck deep enough, it begins to suggest the *religious* priority of life as its corollary.

But that is as far as the dictionary takes us, even in its 1991 printing. Following the old nineteenth-century tradition, it gives special authority to datable literary citations, whereas my argument turns mainly upon colloquial idioms; and in any case, the *OED* is also notably weak on those writers who have been most prominent in our own argument. Lawrence and Leavis in particular are currently very much out of fashion and out of favour, at the very time when their sense of life has suddenly prevailed.

The Dictionary's caution about idioms (or 'phrases', its preferred term) is understandable. Idioms are relatively much more difficult to demonstrate and to date. As I have found in attempting to date the ones that I have quoted, a literary citation is often the best evidence that can be found for the currency of an idiom. Thus the Cambridge lawyer Glanville L. Williams's book-title *The Sanctity of Life and the Criminal Law* (US 1956, UK edn. 1958) is not only the earliest use of **the sanctity of life** I know, but also it probably presupposes that the phrase had recently become current at the time when the book was being written. From the same period, Ian Fleming's *You Only Live Twice* can presumably be taken as hard evidence for the prior currency of **You only live once**. As for **lifestyle**, the new replacement for morality, I recorded its recent arrival in *The Leap of Reason*, 1976.

Without such literary evidence, one can make mistakes. I felt sure that I hear everything, and that I had *not* heard **Get a life** before 1997 – until I found it in a dictionary of idioms published a year or two years earlier than that. Why had I not heard it? Further, I now suspect that it was used in the USA for a few years before its appearance in Britain: Richard Rorty echoes it in an essay first published in 1991.[3]

More recently, the *New Oxford Dictionary of English* has appeared (edited by Judy Pearsall; Oxford: The Clarendon Press 1998). It is determinedly up-to-date, and has about a dozen of my idioms in very much less space than the bigger Oxford Dictionaries have. But even it fails to report any idioms that credit life with special value or sanctity.

With due caution, then, I stick with the view that a body of new idioms that have come into use this past forty years – or less – does embody a fairly coherent religious philosophy of life. One might say that in **the university of life**[4] one is given an unusually good and up-to-date religious education (at least, compared with what you are offered in more conventional academies). Various writers – Continental philosophers and English-language novelists and poets – of the past 150 years or so were the prophets of our new sense of life. Its remoter sources go far back into pagan and biblical antiquity, but its most novel and striking feature is its unprecedentedly high religious valuation just of *life*. In its most realistic form, it seems to postulate some sort of Life-force, an entity about which I personally am sceptical, but even in its non-realist form it is still the vehicle for the expression of very intense religious feelings. As I write (in June 1998) there has been held in London a memorial service for a vegetarian celebrity. Outside in Trafalgar Square the faithful kept vigil with candles and placards saying 'Saint Linda'. The religion of life is currently acquiring its saints, as well as its prophets and teachers. Was Albert Schweitzer its John the Baptist?[5] He probably was; but he too is out of fashion, and his own ethic of Reverence for Life is largely forgotten even as it has prevailed.

I now raise the question: Is the ordinary person's informally-evolved religious philosophy of life, embodied in a stock of new idioms which have become current during the past forty years or so, as rational and as workable as the much more highly-developed systems of belief that are put forward by the religions, and by individual philosophers and theologians? Do those who profess to teach us have anything to offer us that is significantly better than the accumulated folk-wisdom of ordinary language?

In practice, it looks as if the ordinary person is much wiser than the professionals. Because there is no ready-made objective Truth in these matters, the ordinary person makes do with a communally-developed stock of guiding idioms, proverbs, quotations and suchlike, calling upon the one that is most apt and helpful on each occasion, as need arises. They add up to the contemporary person's version of what in the Bible is called 'wisdom literature'.[6] But nothing says that the whole stock of maxims *has* to add up to an orderly system of truth, and the popular wisdom always includes a few sayings that are *prima facie* inconsistent with each other. You are not obliged to use any particular idiom, but you are free to make use of any of them that you find helpful. And this may be a good thing, if life itself is unsystematic, tumultuous and ever-changing.

Furthermore, we have seen that 'the ordinary person's informally-evolved religious philosophy of life, embodied in a stock of idioms which have mostly become current during the past forty years or so' is a very recent formation. It reflects the massive cultural changes that have taken place and have been digested since the early nineteenth century; and as such it seems to be doing very much better than any of our great religions. They are notoriously reluctant to adapt to change, whereas it seems that the people are quick – much quicker than the professionals. Out in the public world new idioms are subject to a process of sifting, because they can spread and become established only if they prove themselves useful to many ordinary people in daily life. Good new idioms catch on very quickly – and that is presumably why ordinary language is more up-to-date than the Academy.

The thesis that ordinariness is all we have for bedrock, and that philosophy ought to pay attention to ordinary language and the ordinary person's vision of the world, is familiar but is in practice disregarded. The thesis that theologians and religious thinkers should pay attention to the religious sensibility and the valuations that are embedded in the idioms of ordinary language is so academically and ecclesiastically unsound that I think nobody has ever yet been foolish enough to put it forward.

I suggest an analogy: the process of natural selection produces tougher, livelier animals than are produced by artificial selection; and in the same way the ordinary person's stock of popular wisdom, tried out in life and gradually taken into the language, is tougher and probably more useful than the artificial systems of thought produced by specialists in academic hothouses.

But where in that case do I fall, and where does this book fall? I think I must reply that in this work of 'democratic philosophy of religion' I am simply reporting – and interpreting —the arrival in our language of a body of new idioms which, taken together, are evidence of a major shift in religious sensibility. However, one friend comments that 'Life-talk can be as naïve, superstitious and self-serving as can God-talk'. He adds that, worse, 'There is a tendency in life-talk to tip over into a very destructive social Darwinism or vitalism which associates life with force, will-to-power, destiny'. And he wants to know whether I am going to produce any *criteria for evaluating* all this new(ish) life-talk. He says I need to do more than merely describe the new idioms.

I think my reply has to be, broadly, Wittgensteinian. I'll say that the stock of idioms made available to us by ordinary language is something so fundamental to the culture that I don't quite know how I could find a superior standpoint from which to pass judgment upon it, with the aim perhaps of expurgating it. All I can suggest is that we should look at and try to understand what it is, how it has arisen, and how it is still developing. That way, we can learn something very deep about how we and our world are presently changing. I'm not telling you what you ought to be thinking, but I am telling you something interesting about a new range of possible thoughts that the current state of the language has made readily accessible to everyone. You may then consider which of these new idioms you have used, or might use, yourself. And it can fairly be said on their behalf that because each idiom has been used by many people and so rubbed smooth, they are *not* in fact particularly superstitious, naïve or self-serving.

Nor do they have to be read metaphysically. Another friend comments that 'one of Derrida's main achievements is to identify this modern theology of life as the final refuge of metaphysics . . . he sets out to deconstruct the metaphysics of life, from Husserl's faith in living consciousness onwards . . .'

That seems to be so. But in no.3 of my fourteen-point summary of 'bio-theology', I have quoted idioms which recognize the possibility of a non-realist view of life, and I would reply to Derrida that my 'solar living' is a purely-expressive and non-metaphysical affirmation of life. In its light, all the idioms can be read as voicing our attitudes, rather than giving us information about an entity called 'life'.

5

But what is Life?

'Life' would have delighted Socrates. He'd have fastened upon it with relish, because it is such a good example of a word whose meaning everyone feels quite sure about – until they are asked to pause for a moment and explain it. Then they suddenly find themselves at a loss. Why? Because it is as if *life has gone cosmic*. The connotation of the word has spread out so far and wide that it seems to have become equivalent to *It all, All this* or *Everything*. The expression **real life** in daily use is equivalent to *the real world*, and someone who wants **to see life** wants to *see the world*. Because we humans are apparently the only beings who have a complete world-view, **the life-world**, *die Leben-swelt, our world*, has become in effect *the world*. Life becomes *all this around us*, which we are passing through, and of which we are parts, in a way that tends to become all-inclusive, totalizing and almost pantheistic. In this context, **to have a religious attitude to life, to love life**, and **to enjoy life** is to love everything in general and the whole passing show of existence. It is a universal and objectless, or non-fixated, kind of love.

So it has come about that during the past century or so, life has gradually become *theologized*. We are shaking off the old idea that 'this world' is a bad thing, and that nothing transient deserves religious attention. On the contrary, just the flux of life is what now attracts our devotion. But this devotion is *object-less*: life is not a substance, not an individual thing of any sort, and we begin to see the need for what may be called a 'negative' or indirect bio-theology. In that spirit, we may present now a series of indirect definitions of life, which will show how the word has come to spread out.

Life, then, is:

(i)   What biologists study;

(ii)   What actuaries calculate;

(iii) What a biography is about;

(iv)   What literature in general, and the novel in particular, seeks to capture or to achieve; and

(v)   It All, as seen from a point of view of a living creature such as you or me, who is in it and part of it all, and whose point of view is the *only* wide-ranging point of view there is.

At several of these levels 'life' shows its curious tendency to 'go cosmic'. At level (i) – 'Life is what biologists study' – nobody nowadays is likely to dispute the suggestion that, in a certain basic sense, life is simply the subject-matter of the biological sciences and may be taken to be what biologists say it is. We don't doubt nowadays that in due course the chemistry of life is likely to be completely unravelled, and we think it likely that better theories of how life began than we have now will soon be put forward. But this rather matter-of-fact and secular view of biological life has become general only since the 1950s. The ancient supernaturalist view of the first origin of life was invoked by Darwin himself in the final sentence of *The Origin of Species*:

> There is grandeur in this view of life, with its several powers, having been originally breathed by the Creator into a few forms or into one . . .[1]

Even as late as the 1960s, many biologists had still not wholly abandoned the idea that the theory of evolution by natural selection *presupposes* that there is at least one population already in existence for selection to work on, and therefore cannot be invoked to account for the appearance of the very first living things. It was felt, in the 1960s and even later, that the origin of the first self-replicating molecules, together with the subsequent origin of the first unicellular organisms, is a huge and extraordinary event, very difficult to imagine occurring by natural causes in the relatively brief period of the Earth's history available. In addition, many biologists were unsure that biology could be fully reduced to chemistry. Could you *really* regard a living thing as just a machine, and the whole vast differentiation of life on Earth as having been quite unmotivated by *any* sort of biological appetition or striving?

In short, even many respectable biologists at that time still doubted whether orthodox mechanistic explanation could fully answer the great theoretical questions of biology. Only in the past thirty years has the old 'top-down' view of life finally faded, as the new molecular biology has brought about the triumph of the 'bottom-up' view of life.[2]

The old 'top-down' view of life was an *activity* theory of life. A living being was responsive and active: it was 'automobile', a sort of unmoved mover. In the thought-world of classical and medieval culture, it was customary to trace the source of all motion, all change and all activity in the material world back to souls, to spirits, and ultimately to God. God was the maximally alive being: he was Life itself, and a living creature was then a material body into which the Creator had breathed life. It was matter *vitalized* by the breath of God. Life in general was thus seen as being a supernatural gift, and pictured in terms of breath and fire. Something of these ancient ideas still survives in our idioms, for you live for **as long as there is breath in your body,** and when you **breathe your last,** you **give up the ghost.** At the opposite end of life, in law a new person's life begins when a newborn baby draws its first breath – and notice here that the opposite of *live* (or *quick*) is *still*.

On the ancient 'top-down', 'activity' theory then, *all* life was cosmic. God was above all a *living* God, Christ was himself the Way, the Truth and the Life, and the Holy Spirit of God was the Lord and Lifegiver, or Quickener (the *Zoopoietes*). There was something divine about even just biological life, for it was God who made hinds calve and women conceive. Just recently, the top-down cosmology has finally perished; but people are not willing simply to abandon their old feeling that all life, and especially new life, is miraculous. What we are witnessing today then is the investment with religious significance of the newly-triumphant 'bottom-up' view of life, evolutionary naturalism. Darwin was right, after all: there *is* grandeur in this view of life.

Next, at level (ii), 'Life is what actuaries calculate': it is the span of human existence from birth to death, and by extension the span of existence of anything and everything else. In this sense also, life tends to go cosmic, for two different reasons. First, setting aside the century, which is a rather recent invention,[3] our own human **lifespan** has always supplied us with our chief measure of a substantial period of time, *via* appeal to **living memory**, family history, the generations, the regnal years of kings and so forth. Our whole understanding of time, especially on the large scale, is thus grounded in our awareness of the time of our own lives. When we try to think God's life-time, we compare it with ours: 'one of God's days is like a thousand years on our timescale'.[4] In modern cosmology everything from protons to galaxies has a finite lifespan, but the unit of scientific measurement is still the (human) year. Indeed, it is hard to see how we could have any measure of time at all which is not grounded in the time of our own lives.

Thus life in the sense of human-life-time tends to go cosmic because it is the base from which *all* our ideas about time are projected out. And secondly, life in the sense of a lifespan, a 'chance', tends to go cosmic in another way. For the extended use of a life in games to mean a chance, or another 'go', or innings reminds us of the dreadful finality of this our one and only life, in all its contingency. The actuary (a profession that goes back to the late seventeenth century) sees everything in human life as a matter of probabilities. We are always utterly vulnerable, but we get only one chance. In **real life** there are no second chances and no retakes. This consideration is cosmic, in the sense that it brings an eschatological finality to bear upon every moment of our life. **It's now or never**; it really is, and it always is. Now or never. **This is it.**

At level (iii), 'A life is what a biography is about'; it is 'the whole series of actions and occurrences constituting the history of an individual from birth to death'. Life is not just biological life, and it is not just the timespan of life: it is also the whole content of a life lived, which in principle may include everything that the person in question is known to have heard, said and felt, read and written, done and suffered. It may include anything that has been part of that person's 'world', or 'objectivity', because every person is interwoven with her or his environment. Before the nineteenth century, biography was rather unsystematic and anecdotal. Only a very few writers with a talent for self-revelation, such as Augustine, Petrarch, James Boswell and Jean-Jacques Rousseau, explored the possibilities of psycho-biography and life-history. In the nineteenth century, as better techniques of historical research became readily available, biographies became much fuller and more systematic. But what was portrayed in *The Life and Letters, The Life and Times*, and *The Life and Thought of* was the socially-presented person, the public figure – even, the public monument. It was customary (as in many quarters it still is customary) for the family to destroy materials thought to be too personal, too private for public disclosure. *My Life and Loves* did indeed exist – but only as underground literature. One might say that in nineteenth-century culture (which in Britain means until the day before yesterday) there was a very sharp distinction between two realms, one public and the other private, one cultural and the other natural, one the world of one's public life and self-presentation and the other the private sphere of biological and in particular sexual life.

How did the distinction come to be broken down? One might cite such things as the readiness of a few bold spirits like the young John Stuart Mill to campaign publicly for 'neo-Malthusianism' (i.e. the diffusion of contraceptive knowledge and techniques) and the rising status of the medical profession and the entry of women into it. But from our present linguistic point of view the most vivid indicator is the arrival in common speech after about 1913 of the phrase **the facts of life**, in the new context of sex education for young people. In the later nineteenth century 'the facts of life' meant merely the harsh conditions of existence in the slums or in the jungle. But through the work of the Eugenics Society and the early twentieth-century sexual reformers **the facts of life** very quickly came to mean facts about sex which obviously ought not to be kept hidden from the young. The phrase may sound comical now, but it still has a ring of protest about it. Its use marks the beginning of general public recognition that just ordinary biological and sexual life should no longer suffer repression and social exclusion. By the late 1990s it had at last become possible for government ministers to be openly and unremarkably gay, and to appear in public with partners to whom they were not married. Biography remains a very popular literary form, and it is now taken for granted that the sexuality of the subject is a proper subject for the biographer even in the case of the most exalted figures of all, such as Einstein and Wittgenstein.

The modern biographer is thus a post-Darwinian biographer, who in writing a life must somehow do justice to and unify all the wide-ranging meanings and uses of 'life' – biological and sexual life, the whole timespan of life, social and communicative life, and purely intellectual life. To attempt to unify all these things and more in a single narrative is to attempt something religious and 'deep', as one might acknowledge in a case such as Ray Monk's philosophical biography of Wittgenstein.[5]

And, I should add, I am *not* talking merely about a 'warts-and-all' type of portrait. I am talking about a religiously-integrated and holistic view of our life.

Which brings us to level (iv), 'Life is what literature in general, and the novel in particular, seeks to be about or to achieve'. Here the most interesting text known to me is Virginia Woolf's essay on 'Modern Fiction', written in April 1919, and already referred to in chapter 2, above.

The essay begins by asking what is wrong with certain very popular contemporary novelists, namely H. G. Wells, Arnold Bennett and John Galsworthy. These writers are excellent observers of the human scene, and very capable craftsmen. All the details are right: so what is missing? Why is it that in the end we don't really *care* about these characters? They leave us with a feeling of triviality. Is life like this? Must novels be like this?

Can it be that . . . Mr Bennett has come down with his magnificent apparatus for catching life just an inch or two on the wrong side? Life escapes; and perhaps without life nothing is worth while . . .[6]

. . . the form of fiction most in vogue at the moment more often misses than secures the thing we seek. Whether we call it life or spirit, truth or reality, this, the essential thing, has moved off . . .[7]

. . . Life is not a series of gig-lamps symmetrically arranged; life is a luminous halo, a semi-transparent envelope surrounding us from the beginning of consciousness to the end.[8]

What is this halo, this semi-transparent envelope? I think Woolf means something that will be very familiar to others who like her are psychologically fragile: the constant consciousness of one's own turbulent physiology, its idiosyncrasy, its productivity of language, its mysteriousness, its strange violence. This is what she seems to be describing when she turns to praise the young James Joyce on the basis of some passages from *Ulysses* that she has read in the *Little Review*:

In contrast with those whom we have called materialists, Mr Joyce is spiritual; he is concerned at all costs to reveal the flickerings of that innermost flame which flashes its messages through the brain . . . The scene in the cemetery, for instance, with its brilliancy, its sordidity, its incoherence, its sudden lightning flashes of significance, does undoubtedly come so close to the quick of the mind that, on a first reading at any rate, it is difficult not to acclaim a masterpiece. If we want life itself, here surely we have it.[9]

Modern fiction, Woolf suggests, needs to be psychological. One needs to watch for the unique way in which, in each person, the flickering flame of the life-impulse turns into language running through the brain. It is above all the great Russians who show us the modern novelist as a saint of life:

In every great Russian writer we seem to discern the features of a saint, if sympathy for the sufferings of others, love towards them, endeavour to reach some goal worthy of the most exacting demands of the spirit constitute saintliness.[10]

Saintliness, however, should not be thought of as involving withdrawal from life. In a later essay, 'Life and the Novelist', Woolf feels an almost Nietzschean desire to catch life on the wing, the newly-minted metaphor and the mood of the moment. One shouldn't 'retire to one's study in fear of life': it is better to be 'terribly exposed to life', even 'a slave to life'. The novelist has to take risks: 'everything is the proper stuff of fiction, every feeling, every thought; every quality of brain and spirit is drawn upon; no perception comes amiss'.[11]

Virginia Woolf's understanding of the novelist's task is a little like that which our own generation associates with Iris Murdoch. The novel – 'our best totalizing medium' as Murdoch has called it – can be about anything and everything. Life too, being what novels are about, can be seen as being anything and everything. But Woolf more importantly has also a much narrower negative bio-theology. Life is a mysterious inner flame within each person: it is an outpouring energy, turning into language. It is the seat of individuality. But it cannot be pointed out. To get at it requires psychological insight, the moral sympathy of a saint, and the patience and discipline of art. It is the one thing needful, *unum necessarium*, the religious object.[12]

Virginia Woolf's account here may be contrasted with Lawrence's 1914 attempt to spell out his own life-philosophy in the unpublished *Study of Thomas Hardy*.[13] Lawrence compares Hardy with Sophocles, Shakespeare and Tolstoy: in these greatest of all writers the little human morality-play is surrounded and dwarfed by 'the terrific action of unfathomed nature', 'the vast uncomprehended and incomprehensible morality of nature or of life itself, surpassing human consciousness'.[14] In Sophocles and Shakespeare the vast uncomprehended order crushes the tragic hero who dares to challenge it, whereas in Hardy and Tolstoy the little human morality crushes the hapless woman or man who transgresses it.

It is very notable that in these two more recent writers the greater background order, though still present, has become impassive: it does not *act*, and classical tragedy is evidently no longer possible. But in any case, Lawrence is not quite a follower either of Shakespeare and Sophocles, or of Hardy and Tolstoy. Like Nietzsche, he has a gospel to preach. He has an immanent, vitalistic idea of life, and a desire to launch out upon it and trust it. His argument is not readily accessible to someone who has had a conventional training in philosophy, but it appears to run something like this: Life is an end in itself, and perhaps indeed our chief end. We don't live to eat, we eat in order to live; and we shouldn't live to work, we should work only enough to be able to embark on the greater business of living. For Lawrence the world of work is the world of mechanical repetition: routines, technology, knowledge, 'proven and deposited experience', 'the past of life'. In the end, it is a prison. Like Caesar in the Gospel, it has to be given its due – 'three or four hours a day', perhaps[15] – but then a human being must claim the freedom to live. And to live is to grow into the future, into the unknown. 'For real utter satisfaction, a human being must give himself up to complete quivering uncertainty, to sentient non-knowledge'.[16] Just as there used to be a mystical non-knowledge of God, so for Lawrence there is a directly-felt mystical non-knowledge of *life*.

Lawrence doesn't deny that there is contentment in work. A craftsman 'becomes one with the old habitual movement: he is the perfect machine, the perfect instrument: he works. But, satisfied for the time being of that which has been and remains now finite, he wearies for his own, limitless being, for the unresolved, quivering, infinitely complex and indefinite movement of new living, he wants to be free' – free to be himself, and to produce himself.[17]

Woolf and Murdoch link life-talk with loving attention to the 'inner flame' that makes the other person the unique living individual that she or he is; whereas Lawrence's life-talk is more often associated with a desire to venture out into the unknown.

Finally (v), 'Life is It All, as seen from the point of view of a living creature such as you or me, who is immersed in it and part of it all'. The fact that we look at life from a standpoint within life, being ourselves living creatures who are always inside our own livingness, means that we cannot have an *objective religious* understanding of life. The religious kind of understanding always involves the self, and our religious desire to know life is also and always a quest for self-knowledge. Hence Virginia Woolf's metaphor of a 'semi-transparent envelope': our own livingness is the framework within which we must operate. This makes life sort-of theological, in the sense that it is both within us and all around us. Thus, once again life has gone cosmic, and we glimpse something of how and why the meaning of 'life' has been expanding so that it can come – in part at least – to fill the gap left by God.

Our language here suddenly brings us very close to the language of the young Hegel, whose manuscript *The Spirit of Christianity and Its Fate* was probably written at Frankfurt in 1798/99. Hegel sees in Jesus' gospel of love an attempt to overcome religious alienation – that is, the subjection of the believer to an infinite sovereign Lord who stands objectively over against us: 'To this infinite field of lordship and bondage there can be opposed only the pure sensing of life which has in itself its justification and authority . . . Since the divine is pure life, anything and everything said of it must be free from any implication of opposition'.[18] Hegel even equates life with being – 'Pure life is *being*'[19] – and with spirit, and with pure self consciousness.

It is a very striking thought that in today's life-talk we modern Anglo-Saxons may at last be following in Hegel's footsteps. Is our new 'bio-theology' something like a postmodern theology of spirit?

A curiosity: in both the old metaphysics and the old theology there was already a promise that an absolute, perspectiveless vision of the world did exist, and could in some way be attained by us. A ready-made, objective truth of things was out-there, waiting to be copied in our knowledge. It would deliver us from the limitations imposed on us by our own finitude, our needs and our passions. But when we move over to the immanent vision of the-world-as-life we perforce give up the old dream of absolute, perspectiveless knowledge, and the novel – together with such related forms as drama, cinema, opera and so forth – becomes the most accessible medium for exploring the questions of life. That much, we can all accept. *But what about science?* The majority of scientists appear to cling obdurately to the old belief in absolute or objective knowledge. They agree that theology and metaphysics do not give us such knowledge, but they believe that in well-established theories of natural science we do have a large body of objective knowledge about the world which is *not* relativized by our language, nor by the structure of our sense organs, nor by our temporality, nor even by the way that what counts as knowledge has changed historically and will presumably continue to change.

However, scientific activity and scientific knowledge do not inhabit an independent world of their own. Science always presupposes and is constructed within the life-world (as Husserl says), which is the world of ordinary language (as Wittgenstein says). This world of everyday life and ordinary language is, in Husserl's phrase, 'the uninvestigated horizon' of the natural sciences. It is compulsory for us, in the sense that we cannot opt out of it: it is, so-to-say, *humanly* necessary. But it is not *metaphysically* absolute or necessary, and indeed over the centuries it very slowly develops historically. One day, perhaps, we'll try to write 'horizon-history', the history of our *a priori* truths, our paradigms and our inescapable presuppositions.

Meanwhile, the survival even into postmodernity of scientific dogmatism is a puzzle, and gives rise to paradoxes. For example (a), let us grant that scientific realism is true and that we are fully justified in taking a strongly-realistic view of the truth of our own current scientific theory. Then (b), we must judge that the great bulk of what passed for scientific knowledge 500 years ago was objectively simply erroneous. But (c), the development of science is more rapid today than ever, and will doubtless continue to be very rapid. *A fortiori*, then (d), people 500 years hence will surely be fully justified in judging that the great bulk of what passes for scientific knowledge today is objectively simply erroneous. But now, how can we today both know that we are all right (when we make one comparison) and know that we are all wrong (when we make another)? How can we be, 'realistically' or objectively, both all right and all wrong at once? Or, to put the point more simply and less combatively, how can knowledge *both* have a history *and* be 'objective' or 'absolute' in the old, strong Platonic sense?

In reply to this sort of puzzle, a person who sees the-world-as-life can reasonably take a pragmatist view of science, and simply offer an historical explanation of why different scientific theories can fit experience and seem right in different historical periods.[20] One can just as well love science and do science without being a scientific realist as one can love religion and practise religion without being a theological realist. Scientists do not need to cling to the old theological dream of absolute knowledge. They should give it up.

And that's that.

6

Life, Being and God

In mythology Proteus, the herdsman of Neptune, could not be captured because he was able continually to elude his pursuers by changing his shape.

So it is nowadays with the religious object. The old metaphysical theism has decayed, and society has become very much more pluralistic than it was even as recently as the nineteenth century. There is no longer just one canonical religious vocabulary, socially established and in good working order. And, in addition, the old religiously-backed value-scales have at many points been reversed. So the philosopher and the religious writer find themselves trying to fix their own personal vocabulary and to paint their own personal portrait of the religious object. But then one finds that, like Proteus, the religious object changes shape and slips away even as one is trying to get it pinned down.

Some people will find this account irritating. As they see it, the traditional religious object – namely, the God of some historic version of Islam, Christianity or Judaism – is still *there*, securely in place. They find any sort of revisionism odious, and even incomprehensible. They just don't see what someone like me is trying to do.

Perhaps the best answer I can give is to say again that we live at a time when the religious object is undergoing complex processes of transformation. In what is going on at least four different strands – four different pressures upon thought – can be made out.

There is, *first*, the gradual, painful transition from a realist to a non-realist account of the religious object. This converts the religious object into what Kant calls an Ideal: it is a postulate, an *as if* to live by, a guiding star and an imaginary focus of aspiration; a hope, a dream and a symbol of perfection.

Secondly, there is the impulse to get rid of the old two-level account of reality, abolishing the Better World Above and bringing the religious object fully down into nature, into history, and into the evolving process of this world.

Thirdly, there is a desire to dissolve away many of the traditional infinite divine attributes, and especially the attributes of necessity of being, immutability, impassibility, and omnipotent sovereignty. In fact, *omnipresence* seems to be the only infinite attribute we really want to keep.

And *fourthly*, we want the religious object to lose its proper Name – by which I mean all those features that are held to give one particular human community a privileged relation to it.

These four themes are powerful imperatives that have motivated many religious thinkers in the period since the times of Spinoza,[1] Kant and Hegel. But they are not fully compatible with each other, and it is the interplay between them that now generates so many and varied accounts of the religious object. In particular, there is a tension between the Kantian tendency to make God into a pure ideal or standard, and the Hegelian tendency to merge God into the unfolding process of the world.

It was for this reason that (as I have suggested elsewhere) the work of Kant quickly produced a situation after 1800 in which different contemporary thinkers could be found resolving God down into either morality, history, nature or Christ.[2] Kant himself had resolved the relation between ourselves and God into the relation between our conscience and the demand of *the moral law*; and many others subsequently followed him. Hegel and his historicist successors – including the Marxists – resolved our relation to God into our relation to the whole march of *History* as it moves towards its coming totalization. Schleiermacher and the Romantics resolved the relation to God into a feeling-response of the heart to the *Whole* in which we live and move and have our being. The Transcendent is relaunched as the Sublime. And fourthly, Blake and the radical Protestant tradition resolve the relation to God down into faith's response to *Christ*, Jesus Christ himself being the only Way to God, and so in effect the only God.

I have personal experience of this protean quality of the modern religious object, for in my own writing the religious object has in successive periods been presented as *the Unknown God of the negative theology*; as a pure *guiding spiritual ideal*; as non-language, the efflux of pure formless contingency, Being; and as the twentieth-century's new and religiously-revalued meaning of *Life*. Don't blame me for changing God. I didn't change very much. What happened was that the religious object changed as I wrote.

These eight different reinterpretations of God seem to fall into two main groups. The first group (*the moral law, the unknown God, the guiding spiritual ideal*) strive to keep a vestige of the old idea that the religious object is something authoritative and unchanging that transcends the flux of this world. Even when no longer thought of as a real personal being, God is still in a sense up-there. The second group of reinterpretations (*the Goal of History, Nature, Being, Life*) abandon metaphysics and gradually learn to find divinity just in the way the flux of things continuously comes forth, gives itself to us and carries us along. Faith is then to accept your historical situation and task, to accept your own pure contingency without anxiety, and to **say Yes to life**.

As for the reduction of God to Christ only, much will depend upon how the term 'Christ' is interpreted. It might mean a Kantian timeless ideal of perfect Manhood, or it might be used in the sense of any bare fork'd animal, any ordinary Joe like you or Homer Simpson or me. Nowadays I use the term only in the latter of these two senses; as Everyman or anyone.

But this polymorphism of the religious object prompts the question: what *is* religion, and what sort of object or goal *should* it be looking to? Just how objective – how much of a being out there – does the religious object need to be?

There seem to be *four* main classes of answer to this question.

(a) In the standard *theistic realism* of classical Christianity and Islam the religious object was regarded as a real being, an infinite spiritual substance (or bodiless mind) with at least some personal attributes. And this objective absolute reality of God was and is considered by believers to be essential, a *sine qua non* for religion.

(b) In various forms of *pantheism and religious naturalism* the religious object may be an encompassing milieu in which we participate, and which sustains and empowers us, such as 'the Whole', or Being, or 'Life'. This object is a sort-of Other to which we can relate ourselves, but it is not an individual being in I-Thou *apposition* to us.

(c) In *Christian non-realism* and in some forms of religious existentialism the religious object is an imagined guiding star, a fictioned, 'poetical' or ideal object of aspiration. Like a hope or an ambition, it is something that we cherish in our hearts and which guides our conduct.

(d) In various forms of *mystical and meditation religion* the religious object is simply a state of oneself (or perhaps better, a state into which the self passes and becomes rapt). This state may be described in terms of blessedness, liberation from all evil and suffering, and personal fulfilment. Or we may see it as consisting simply in having a clear, cool and fully-awakened consciousness.

This is a rather coarse sketch of the chief possible ways of picturing the religious object. But it does at least suffice to make the point that we cannot portray the world's various religious traditions as a number of different Ways of moving towards one and the same Divine Goal. It simply cannot be claimed that, for example, Jains and Muslims are making the same journey while wearing different liveries. This idea, popularized by syncretism in antiquity and by Vivekananda and others in modern times, is thoroughly confusing. The metaphor of a *journey* is particularly misleading, for nobody now would wish to portray the religious object as being far off. The language of going on a journey to seek God doubtless originated at a time when gods had individual temples, and you went on a pilgrimage to a particular shrine in order to 'seek the face' of a particular god. But nobody today quite does that. The religious object may have very varying degrees of objectivity, but I think virtually everyone today would see it as being 'omnipresent', or universally accessible. Everyone and everything is equally close to it. We do not need to travel in order to attain it; all we need to do is to change our habits of thinking and feeling.

This now invites the question: But do we need to have a religious object *at all*? I have confessed to a personal movement from (a) to (c), and then to (b) with a dash of (d). Am I then a Cheshire Cat, fading away? For you may say that if I'm talking about the religious object's ceasing to be pictured as the Real God out-there of classical theistic metaphysics, so that God is internalized within us as a inner guiding spiritual Ideal, and then at a later stage is demythologized still further so that our relation to God becomes simply our relation to It-All or Being, or Life, then surely religion is steadily vanishing as a distinct 'concern' and sphere of life? Surely, if religion is to continue as a fairly distinct social institution and sphere of life, it needs to have a relatively-distinct object or *telos*? But if God is melted down into everything in general, there's no reason why religion should continue to be anything in particular.

We are not talking here only about the movement from a realistic to a non-realist account of God, because the disappearance of religion as a distinct concern may currently be threatened even in Buddhism – despite the fact that Buddhism is already pragmatist and non-realist *to start with*, and therefore might be thought to be unworried by the scepticism of the modern West. No: Buddhism is threatened too, by those westernizing Buddhist writers who seek to demythologize away its religious content and interpret Buddhist meditation simply as mind-therapy – a way to gain a clear and easy consciousness, unclouded by anxiety or egoism, that is happy to see everything as it is and for what it is.[3] This awakened, 'cosmic' sort of consciousness is a great blessing: but once we've reached it, it surely becomes just a secular fact? Might not the very same happy result be achieved by a good scientific education, or even just by relaxation exercises?

Do you see the difficulty? The demystifier seeks to purify

religion and make it universal by extracting it from metaphysics
and from its 'Hebrew old clothes'. But the result may be that
religion, like the disappearing Jew in today's America, simply
vanishes happily by disappearing into secularity. Is that what
we were after? When we were talking about the various trans-
formations that the religious object has been undergoing in
modern times, perhaps what we were really describing was its
gradual disappearance? And when we get to the point where the
religious object is no more than just the purely-contingent flux
of Being, or 'life' in general, surely 'radical theology' has
reached its furthest possible extreme. Next stop – nothingness,
disappearance, silence.

I don't agree, for in the curious new religious situation in
which we now find ourselves, there is still the old Problem of
Evil, albeit in a new form. In a developed modern economy, life
has been made very predictable and secure for most people most
of the time. Most of us can expect everything to work out
satisfactorily for us, and that we will live rather longer than the
biblical allotted span of seventy years. People have come to
expect peace and prosperity as of right, and are increasingly
inclined to look for someone to blame and to sue when anything
at all goes wrong for them. In a democracy we elect people to
make sure that everything goes right for us, and if they fail us
we fire them.

As a result we have become quite astonishingly eudaemonistic. In the old religious order, people were assured that a good
God watched over them and would protect them from evil.
When things went wrong, they complained bitterly to God.
That was the old problem of evil. In the new developed con-
sumer society, people expect the whole régime of management
– political, economic, technological, medical – to look after
them very efficiently. Everybody has a right to happiness, and a
right to assume that the system will deliver and protect them
from harm. And this modern expectation of near-invulnerability
is even stronger than the old expectation of divine protection,
with good reason. After all, the new system has already
succeeded in delivering much longer, securer, and more

prosperous lives than people ever enjoyed in the past. All the more outrage and indignation, then, when something goes badly wrong. People feel that they have been let down. They demand 'justice', by which they mean satisfaction, which means a full public enquiry, followed by compensation for them, punishment for those whose negligence permitted disaster to strike, and measures to ensure that such a thing never happens again.

Under the old religious order that prevailed on the whole until the early nineteenth century, people expected God to look after them: under the new technological/consumerist order people expect the system to look after them. In both orders the eudaemonistic assumption is the same: I am one of the righteous, the good people, and I have a right to expect that things will go well for me. The whole system of things is *for me*; it revolves around me, and its job is to look after my interests and protect me from harm.

So the problem of evil arises in much the same way under the old order and in the new, and it is a problem of disappointed expectations. People have been too ready to believe false promises and to forget Being – which means, to forget life's utter contingency. You'll only be able fully to appreciate life's religious depth, its beauties, its demand and its joys if you fully accept its contingency. For, of course, anyone may suddenly find themselves with a handicapped child, a motor accident, a cancer, or a breakdown of one sort or another. And there will be nobody to blame. **That's nobody's fault. It's just life** (quoted from Dea Birkett, *The Guardian*, 8 July 1998). Here, ordinary language uses the word 'life' to remind us that the world is not a nursery. There is *not* a moral world-order. Nobody has pre-arranged everything for our benefit. It's **a hard life**: meaning that everything comes at us strange, wonderful and very chancy. We can certainly love it and have faith in it, but it gives us no guarantees whatever. As Spinoza remarked, we are not loved back.

Interestingly, in the old Catholic theology the most prominent of the proofs for the existence of God was the argument *e*

contingentia mundi, from the utter contingency of the world
and everything in it. We keep that sense of religious wonder
at everything's sheer contingency. The purely contingent
givenness-to-us of our life and everything in it arouses a sense of
wonder and non-objective gratitude. And we feel that religious
wonder at life all the more keenly and clearly when we have
forgotten the bad Thomistic philosophy that used to argue
both that everything is contingent and perishing *and* that it is
impossible that *everything* should be contingent and perishing,
so that *therefore* there must be something that is eternal and
immutable, namely God.

So we keep the religious wonder at 'life' or existence, but we
abandon the bad philosophy, and we also abandon the eudaemonistic assumption that the whole course of things has been,
and *must* have been, prearranged for our benefit. We still live
the old life of faith, but out in the open now, and without any
of the old dogmatic guarantees. There is no metaphysical order
behind the flux of appearances, from which any guarantees
might emanate. There is no absolute Being and there is no
absolute Nothingness. There is only life. There is only the life-
world and life's self-affirmation. Life has no outside, and there
is not anywhere where the dead are: that is why nowadays the
only thing we can do on behalf of the dead is **to remember them
as they were in life,** and celebrate their lives. Since there is
nothing outside life, there is no other way in which we can
connect with them, or do anything for them, except simply to
cherish their memory.

To say that there is only life is to say that everything is
contingent. There is contingent being, and there is contingent
non-being. So the only ontological line we draw is that between
the possible and the (contingently) actual. Along this line fluctu-
ations or ripples dance, as things come into existence and pass
away again. Life is, then, just this dance along the line between
the possible and the actual. And on the view of religion I am
proposing, a true religious acceptance of the contingency of life
is the best cure for the false eudaemonistic kind of religion that
many people profess, and which in the end lets them down so

badly. When we have given up the last vestige of belief in, or desire for, 'life after death'; when we fully appreciate the out-sidelessness of life, *then* we begin to see life's religious meaning with open eyes.

The image of our human creaturely existence as a dance or a tightrope walk over the void of non-being[4] is old, and has very often been invoked within the Christian tradition. So we still invoke it; but more seriously than our predecessors, who first cited it – and then fell back upon dogmatic guarantees. Our life is *both* radically contingent *and* outsideless. It's all there is.

To grasp the implications of this, we take up another old and familiar image of human life, from Bede. In about the year AD 627, King Edwin of Northumbria is holding a council in his big wooden hall – its post-holes have now been found, near Kirk Yetholm – about whether he and his realm should embrace the Christian faith. One counsellor says:

> The present life of man, O king, seems to me, in comparison of that time which is unknown to us, like to the swift flight of a sparrow through the room wherein you sit at supper in winter, with your commanders and ministers, and a good fire in the midst, while storms of rain and snow prevail abroad; the sparrow, I say, flying in at one door, and immediately out at another, whilst he is within, is safe from the wintry storm; but after a short space of fair weather, he immediately vanishes out of your sight, into the dark winter from which he had emerged. So this life of man appears for a short space, but of what went before, or what is to follow, we are utterly ignorant. If therefore this new doctrine contains something more certain, it seems justly to deserve to be followed.[5]

This image makes human life seem short, in comparison with what came before it, and what is to come after it. But if our life really is outsideless, then the image of a dark wintry vastness outside, about which religion may give us important informa-tion, is deeply misleading. We don't come into this life from another place or a previous form of life, outside it: we just begin. And when we die we do not leave the stage and pass away to another region beyond it: we just cease to be. There is no place or duration external to life by comparison with which our lifespan can be described as either long or short. Furthermore, the relation of before and after between one thing or event and another holds only *within* life. It cannot be invoked to relate something *within* life to some other order *outside* life.

Thus our life just is what it is, and is what we make it; and we can do without the cliché about the brevity of life. 'It's not *that* short!', snapped the late Marghanita Laski in conversation with me once. And she was right. The religious stimulus comes, not from life's brevity, but from the *absence* of any external yardstick or basis of comparison, and from the fact that you get only one take. There are no retakes. The clock cannot be put back. Nobody can step in the same river twice. You can't go home again. There is no exact repetition. Everything happens only once.

What is religious, awesome and demanding about life is this combination of trembling contingency, evanescence, irrevocability, and infinite weight – neatly conveyed in idiomatic English by the question and answer: **Is this it? This is it.**[6] Say those six words with stress on words two, three, four and six. That is the last truth. It's all there is to say.

* * *

The question now arises: at different times I have described the religious object as God (understood in a non-realistic way, as a pure guiding spiritual ideal), as Being, and as Life. How are these three representations of the religious object related to each other? Which do I *really* believe in?

To which I answer that we really *do* live after the end of metaphysics – which means that we can no longer suppose that behind the flux of the world there is just one enduring and ultimate truth of things, which can be known by us humans, and can be conveyed in our language. The old belief was typically that the human mind, being made in the image of the divine mind, was apt to know the eternal order; and also that God was a language-user who both had made the world and dictated the text of scripture in a human language. This exceedingly top-down idea of language effectively guaranteed the capacity of a human language to compass and to comprehend the eternal order. But it is not an idea that we can hold today. For us, language evolved from below. In which case we are compelled to regard the great metaphysical systems of the past, and the great systems of religious belief, as being something like the Gothic cathedrals – as being great works of art, and no more than that. Philosophy cannot 'go beyond' art.

It follows that we should see the speculative philosopher and the religious writer as people rather like poets. In each of their works a theory is ridden, metaphors are pressed and themes are developed in order to create a selectively enhanced and illuminating art-image of the human condition. Such an image may significantly change the way people see their worlds and shape their lives. But it should never be fetishized; that is, it should never be made the starting-point for the construction of a fresh system of dogmatic truth. On the contrary, the artist-theologian or artist-philosopher is free to produce more works and to develop new images, without being required to organize them all into one great system of Truth. Indeed, we should give up the idea of dogmatic truth entirely, and instead rely only upon the creativity of the religious imagination.

The religious object, then, may for certain purposes be written as God. For other purposes, it may be written as Being, and for other purposes, it may be written as Life. But, as I have long emphasized, neither God nor Being nor Life is supposed to be a substance – a distinct individual that exists independently of the language in which we talk about it. The position is rather that, when we portray the religious object as God, we represent it as an imaginary focus of spiritual aspiration – an ideal of perfection. When we portray the religious object as Being, we are asking for the abandonment of all ideas of necessity of being and ultimate security, and instead trying to focus religious attention upon the continually-emergent, purely-contingent givenness of all being, to us and in us. And when we portray the religious object as Life we try to find it already present in the common speech of ordinary people. And so it is.

Appendix

The Idioms and the Method

The number of idiomatic phrases about life in British English is very large, and changing all the time. It is certainly possible, and indeed likely, that I have entirely overlooked a number of excellent and relevant phrases. I urge readers to write to me with them, and will try to include them – or at least, the best of them —in the next impression or edition of this book, if one is called for. I will also be glad of good literary citations, because they are not easy to find. But don't write if you are reading this many years after its first publication, because I may be gone, and in any case the present aim is only to capture the philosophy of life that was encoded into common speech during the last few years of the twentieth century.

Before you decide that a particular idiom or quotation is relevant to our present argument, look at it closely. Not long after I had sent off the final version of this book to the publisher, I chanced upon the following sentence: 'Life and language are alike sacred'. It comes from the first of the 'Breakfast Table' sketches of Oliver Wendell Holmes, and was first published in a newspaper in 1857. Taken at face value it is over fifty years too early, and it gave me a nasty shock. Had I entirely missed something very big? Not to worry. Holmes is only saying facetiously that it is as sinful to twist a man's word as it is to wring his neck, that's all.

* * *

How far does all the argument of this book apply to other countries and languages – for example, to American English, and to French and German? Dictionaries indicate that German has a rich vocabulary of idioms expressing *lebenslust* (a word that recalls Chaucer's use of *lustie*) and, peasantlike, is especially rich in uses of life to mean a livelihood, a living, a subsistence. As for American English, one is aware of cultural differences: for example, the British bury soldiers where they fall, so that the relatives are inevitably made aware of visiting young bones, and of going back in time. The dead person has not grown old as we that are left grow old. So the British think of the dead person as *a life* that is now in the past. By contrast, the Americans repatriate the bodies of dead soldiers, with the result that the surviving relatives are able, more easily perhaps, to settle their dead, *as* the dead, in the corporate memory that we call the past. And more generally, it may be that current American English embodies a slightly different popular wisdom of life. Maybe the idea that all truth and value are mediated to us by 'life' comes to Americans through the Declaration of Independence as constitutive of their whole heritage: 'life, liberty and the pursuit of happiness'. Is the US *constitutively* the first **life-world**? I don't know for sure, and would welcome assistance. Literary references and dates would be most welcome, if they are available.

All that said, I venture the hypothesis that the change from a God-centred to a Life-centred religious vocabulary is such a big and important shift that it is very unlikely to be happening in one country only. As I write, I note that the creation of an informal shrine by laying flowers at a site where a life was suddenly and tragically cut short is reported not only from France, but also from the Capitol in Washington D.C., and from Sweden. And Frank Sinatra has died: was he not the prophet of Nietzscheanism in popular song?

* * *

I subjoin a list of the idioms, nearly all of them very recent, and including the words 'life', 'live' or 'living', that have been quoted in this book in **bold** type as being directly relevant to its argument. They are arranged here in (approximate) alphabetical order, as in a dictionary.

A
An aim in life
An answer to life's riddle
You've got entirely the wrong attitude to life

B
We believe in life before death
Life's a bitch!
The breath of life
A blasphemy against life

C
A Celebration of the Life of . . .
Facing up to life's challenges
A crime against life
Take life as it comes
Coming to life
Commitment to life

D
Live dangerously
To deny life
Despair of life
Distrust of life
Life is not a dress-rehearsal
Domestic life, the sanctity of: and see
    also public life, private life, sex life, double life

E
Living on the edge
Enjoyment of life
Life-enhancing

F
The facts of life
Faith in life
Faithful to life

Fear of life
Feeling more alive / What makes me feel most alive
Fighting for life/to save (another's) life
Something to live for
Life-force
Live fast, die young / Life in the fast lane
Live life to the full, a full life
Full of life
The futility of life

G
Get a life!
Getting more out of life
Getting on in life
The gift of life/take life as a gift
. . . by her death she was able to give life to others
Grateful to life, gratitude for life
Life goes on/must go on
My life isn't going anywhere
Life's been good to me
The good things of life

H
I take my life in my hands
A hard life
Life's hard
Life's been hard on him
He's made life hard for himself
The holiness of life

I
I've had my life
In love with life

J
The joys of life
(That's nobody's fault), it's just life

K
The kiss of life

L
The land of the living
The lessons of life
Life's like that
I want to live my own life
For the life of me
A life to live
Life's a lottery / It's just the luck of the draw / Win some, lose
    some
Life-loving
Lifestyle (c.1973)
To live a lie
Love life while you have it/while it lasts
The love of life
She loved life
Lust for life

M
Life is what you make it
What is the meaning of life?
The miracle of life/of new life
Don't miss out on life
A mission in life
Surely there's more to life than this?
Life must go on
The mystery of life

N
A normal life / I want to get back to living . . .

O
You only live once
Live life one day at a time
You only have one life

P
I feel as if life's passed me by
A path in life/life-path / Walks of life
Perspective upon life
Philosophy of life
Pro Life
I prefer to remember her as she was in life
Purpose in life
Put some life into it!
You only get out of life what you put into it

Q
Quality of life/quality-adjusted life-years
The big questions of life

R
Rage for life
Real life
Respect for life
Today is the first day of the rest of your life
Reverence for life
The right to life
You can't run away from life

S
All life is sacred
The sanctity of life
To save lives
The secret of life
To see life/a bit of life
What life sends
Life's short
A sin against life
A spark of life
Life-stance
Life never stands still; life moves on
A start in life

To sort out one's life
Start living
Stirrings of life
What life has in store for us
That's the story of my life!
Such is life!
Look on the bright side/the sunny side of life

T
That's life!
This life / This is the life! / This is your life
What lessons has life taught you?
The time of your life
Get my life together again
How's life treating you? / Is life treating you badly?
Trust life
True to life/true life

U
Life's apparent unfairness
The university of life (Horatio Bottomley, 1920)
Unworthy to live

V
The value of life
Variety is the spice of life
View of life
A vocation to life

W
Don't waste your life
Way of life
What life's all about
Where life's leading us
Where life's carrying us
You've got your whole life before you
Life-world

The worth of life
A life worth/not worth living

Z
Zest for life

And here I add a list of ten other significant idioms that have been quoted in the main text.

It means the world to us
Where will it all end?
Is this it? / This can't be all there is to it / This is it / That's it
Make the most of the time you have left
It's up to you to make something of it
A mere existence (cf. How are you? – Surviving)
The sanctity of marriage/private life/the home/the family
As long as there's breath in my body
He breathed his last – and gave up the ghost
It's now or never

* * *

I have listed about 150 life-idioms, and now ask myself how it came about that I found and chose just *these*, out of the very much larger total number of idioms about life and living that are currently available in the language. Further, would it have been possible for me to proceed purely empirically, and to construct the current religious philosophy of life that I have described merely by analysing current idioms?

In practice, it seems, nobody is a pure Baconian empiricist. As Darwin says of himself, I needed 'a theory by which to work', and my theory both told me what sort of new idioms to look out for, and also supplied a framework for interpreting them. The theory was suggested by the work of writers like Nietzsche and Lawrence, and proposes that traditional belief in God cannot be just lost. It has to be replaced: and our new religious attitude to life represents a secularization of belief in God that allows us to continue using some of the old vocabulary, and expressing most of the old feelings.

The first great thinker to carry out a secularization of God of this type was Spinoza. His new religious object he calls God-or-Nature (*Deus sive natura*), or God-or-substance. There is, absolutely, but One Eternal self-caused Substance. And it is of course arguable that the Modern revaluation of life began with Spinoza.

Five years or so ago I proposed for my own post-metaphysical version of this theological immanentism the label 'energetic Spinozism', secularizing God into 'the Fountain', reality seen as an outpouring flux of *in*substantial energies and meanings that unceasingly scatters and is lost. (Or perhaps are recycled.) Two years ago, captivated by Heidegger, I used the term Being, or Be-ing, or Be(com)ing, meaning by it simply the pure Empty transience of all existence. Here we are following ordinary language and using the term 'life'.

It's worthwhile to keep changing one's terminology. It helps to keep the reader on his toes, and it helps to discourage the return of dogmatism. I don't *want* to be read dogmatically or to be understood as teaching a system. There is no system out there. I just make it all up.

As for the present argument about data and theory, I end by claiming that the theory was itself partly-inductively arrived at; that it guided me to find an interesting body of material; and that it suggested a strikingly coherent interpretation of the data. Thus far, I claim that my argument stands up: the data that the theory required have appeared, and they have confirmed the theory. What is described as 'radical theology', and is much disapproved of by our betters, has it seems no place in the contemporary university or church, but it has a poetic revenge: it has triumphed in common speech.

* * *

Until recently, the word 'life' looked to be such a colourless, nondescript, ordinary little word that nobody much remarked on the way it was being used. Writing about 'the concept of life', or about a particular writer's use of the word, is still a great rarity.

That is why it has proved so difficult to collect the materials for this book. The dictionaries barely report my idioms, and the literary critics themselves have seldom noticed who are the odd, intriguing users of 'life'. I have noticed that the young Auden's use of the word is almost always very interesting, and have incorporated a few scraps of his verse (without attribution) in the main text. A critic-friend recommended Samuel Beckett and Iris Murdoch, and I have used 'Life has no outside', from Murdoch, on p.78 – but without attribution, for a special reason. Alain de Botton's recent *How Proust can change your life* (London: Picador 1997) itself includes some good life-talk, both drawn and not-drawn from Proust's own text. With Beckett, I have drawn a blank. Indeed, I have not found the sort of discussion of 'life' that I have been looking for even in Stephen Prickett, who is well-known for his writings on *Romanticism and Religion* (Cambridge: Cambridge University Press 1976) and on Wordsworth.

'Life' is such a little word that people have as yet hardly begun to notice its use. Hence my difficulty in collecting materials – and also my difficulty in explaining in what it is that is so *important* about the way our use of the word life has changed and is still changing.

One friendly critic forces the issue by demanding a discussion of life-talk in the Bible and the Western Christian tradition. Am I, he wonders, unreasonably prejudiced against the tradition? I haven't even referred to the distinction in Greek between *zoe* and *bios*.

So I must respond; and it happens that one superlatively thorough and able analysis of 'life' in the Bible and in classical antiquity does exist. It is the long article s.v. '*zao, zoe (bioo, bios) . . .*' in Volume II of G. Kittel's encyclopaedic *Theological Wordbook of the New Testament* (tr. G. W. Bromiley, Grand Rapids, Michigan: Eerdmans 1964). The bulk of the article is by Bultmann, but he hands over to Gerhard von Rad for a section on the Old Testament.

Rudolf Bultmann was not only a very good technical scholar, but also, as a former associate of Martin Heidegger, someone acutely aware that ancient and modern understandings of life are profoundly different. Amongst the ancient Greeks, he remarks, it was indeed well understood that each human being has a human life that is his or her own:

> Yet this thought is not carried through radically. The various human lives (*bioi*) are not regarded as unique and unrepeatable; they are classified and graded in self-repeating types . . . It is not the historical moment, or the claim of the Thou addressed to man in it, which gives man the possibility of true being. What he has to actualise in his individual existence is the supratemporal and general . . . (p.837).

In the Old Testament it is of course acknowledged that I have a life that is mine, and that my destiny depends upon my own choice: by obedience to the law of God or the injunctions of Wisdom I can make sure of a long and happy life, whereas by disobedience I can consign myself to an early death. But what is utterly missing is the idea that by my manner of living I can appropriate my life as my own, forging a unique selfhood and a course of life that is mine only. In Old Testament terms, says Bultmann, 'one may speak of a happy or unhappy life (Psalm 90.10), but one cannot speak of living happily or unhappily, well or badly' (p.851). The ancients had no idea of a **lifestyle**, a distinctive individual manner of conducting one's own life. They had no thought of wanting to **do it my way**.

Even in the New Testament, Bultmann continues, *zoe* is never regarded or investigated as an observable phenomenon (p.863). And now we have enough: we see that life in the sense of 'what the novel is about' is totally absent from traditional religious thought. It simply had not yet been invented. We live *after* Rousseau and Boswell, *after* the Enlightenment and the Romantic Movement, *after* the rise of the life story. For us everything starts with the developing human subject, the human social world, and the ongoing drama of human relationships within which we each and all of us are engaged in producing our lives and forming our selves. For us, the human life-world comes first. It is a world of ceaseless intercourse and business of every kind, and it is very deep. Our most typical art forms – the novel, the feature film, so-called 'bourgeois' drama, soap operas – are devoted to exploring it, helping us to understand it, and equipping us the better to play our own part in it, and to become ourselves within it.

'Life', in this sense, is of course totally absent from the Bible and the main religious tradition. 'Life' is a modern invention; indeed, it is *the* Modern invention. The older tradition started from God, the cosmos and divine Law, before which the human being stood naked. There was no 'life': where we have 'life', they had only certain great moral and religious facts. But with the Enlightenment and the rise of the novel a huge cultural transformation began, and still slowly proceeds. Out of it has emerged our own new sense of life, and the general revaluation of ordinary life that has been coming through in ordinary language in the past generation or so.

Once, the human life-world, so far as it was recognized at all, was merely Vanity Fair. It was 'the world': it was worthless and shallow. One *fled* it. Now it is revalued, and has become very deep. It demands the highest gifts of the greatest artists. And it also demands the rethinking of religion and morality – as for example was attempted by Christian existentialism from Kierkegaard to Bultmann. But as the generations pass, the scale of the redevelopment required gets to look bigger and bigger. Both Kierkegaard and, a century later, Bultmann now seem to have put forward excessively-conservative proposals for reconstruction. This present little essay hopes at least to have got a fair and accurate picture of where we are, by looking at what is currently happening in everyday speech.

* * *

One of my young advisers professes amusement. Cupitt looks at the bedrock rationality, the common sense, that is expressed in the idioms of ordinary language – and there sees his own face. How can this be? If they are right and I am a maverick, an extremist, how can it be that I have found in the new idioms now arriving in everyday speech a point of view so close to my own? Am I the only philosopher of religion who is in touch with **real life**?

There is not really any difficulty here. You may look to other philosophers and theologians for the message you think they think you ought to hear, the message that you expect them to deliver on behalf of the authorities, academic and ecclesiastical, that they speak for. My own aim is somewhat different: I take you on a seemingly roundabout journey in order eventually to reveal to you what you already think. I have heard of people being physically afraid to read my books. Why? Not because I tell you what *I* think, but because I aim to persuade you to acknowledge what, deep down, you know you already think. As George Berkeley long ago put it, philosophy's magical mystery tour circles around and returns into common sense:

> You see, Hylas, the water of yonder fountain, how it is forced upwards, in a round column, to a certain height; at which it breaks and falls back into the basin from whence it rose: its ascent, as well as descent, proceeding from the same uniform law or principle of *gravitation*. Just so, the same principles which at first view lead to scepticism, pursued to a certain point, bring men back to common sense.
>
> (from *The Third Dialogue between Hylas and Philonous*, the concluding words.)

— and 'common sense' is simply an old-fashioned term for the view of things that is embedded in ordinary language. We may try in various ways to get away from it, but in the end we find ourselves coming back to it.

* * *

This essay has used a method new to theology, and almost new to philosophy. We cannot hope nowadays to prove the truth of a system of beliefs in religion or philosophy by rational argument proceeding from self-evident and indubitable premisses.

So I have suggested an alternative method, closer in spirit to Wittgenstein's 'theology as grammar'. I have tried to demonstrate that a certain system of beliefs, a new theology of life, has very recently come to be woven into the fabric of ordinary language, and I have tried to explain how this change has come about. The hope is that you will recognize that this is what you too are coming to think.

The new Life-theology is evidently a secularization of traditional Christian belief – and in particular, belief in God and the everyday 'practice of the presence of God'. It resolves the presence of God down into the feeling of being alive, and it has already affected everyday language and practice so deeply that it has shifted the onus. If you do not acknowledge that the new religiousness of life is now in effect your real religion, the onus is now on *you* to explain how and why you are able to opt out of it in favour of something else.

So I am not saying that I have proved that I'm right, or that the theology of life is dogmatically true. I am saying only that, in Wittgenstein's phrase, *This language-game is played!*: this is how we speak, this is how things now are with us. So – how can you disagree?

How far then might the same method be extended to other areas of philosophy? The prime candidate is one that Wittgenstein would not have considered, namely *ethics*. As has been hinted in the text above, an old moral vocabulary of command and obedience, of conscience and duty, and of law and casuistry, has died in the past forty years or so. As we have remarked, it has been replaced by a new post-Sixties personal morality of self-expression and **lifestyle,** of wanting above else to claim the right to do one's own thing in one's own way – while of course wanting others to enjoy the same expressive freedom too. It's a case of **live and let live.** And during the same period, social morality has become the same thing as politics: it has become the continuing work of brokering peaceful co-existence between different interests, points of view, fundamentalisms and pressure-groups. The new saint of social morality is not the single-issue fanatic or the ideologue, but the democratic politician, the fixer, the flexible compromiser, the problem-solver.

See how in the new world reason still presides, not as an absolute Monarch who promulgates the law, but as a canny chairman who finds a form of words that enables the meeting to come to an amicable conclusion! Reason itself has now become a pragmatist, a temporiser.

Thus the method of the present book might be extended to show how morality has also changed recently, and in the process we could very usefully throw all those vociferous absolutists onto the defensive. The onus will be upon them to *prove* their absolutes. And there are also other areas of philosophy which could be similarly transformed – the theory of knowledge, for example.

Some psychologists are also becoming interested in the project of trying to spell out what our basic conception of the world is, and how we have arrived at it. In *Children Talk about the Mind* (Oxford: Oxford University Press 1995) Karen Bartsch and Henry M. Wellman develop a detailed 'naïve theory of the mind' from taped records of 200,000 conversations between kindergarten-aged children. This again suggests that if it were done sufficiently thoroughly on a large-enough scale, study of ordinary people's talk might come to make a big difference both to theology and to philosophy. And study of how and why such talk is *changing* will be of particular interest.

Wittgenstein and his followers have recognized that the structure of our language commits us to a cosmology. Going further, D. Z. Phillips and others have claimed that the philosophy of religion should be seen as a purely descriptive subject, which spells out the 'logic' or the 'grammar' of *God* and *faith*. But all these people were very reluctant to get involved in historical theology: they haven't wished to discuss how and why our deepest convictions in matters of philosophy, religion and ethics evolve historically. But if the main ideas of the present essay are correct, the present age in which we live is one in which profound and rapid change in belief is taking place and can easily be studied empirically by tracing changes in idiomatic speech.

For over a century scholars have dreamt of a 'science of religion'. They have collected and analysed reports of 'paranormal' events or religious experiences, and they have studied the social psychology of religion. So far at least, the results have been very disappointing; and I think the reason is that they have looked for their data in the wrong place. They have looked for experiences had, or beliefs held, within the murky and uncertain world of individual subjectivity. I have suggested that, on the contrary, we should look at the way language is moving and changing in the common, brightly-lit public world. In the public realm we have a much better hope of agreement about what the data are and how to test theories about them.

* * *

The sharpest comment of all upon the main argument of this book has not yet been made to me, but I'll make it anyway. Language contains many interesting periphrases for God, some of them doubtless originally reverential, such as *the good Lord, the Almighty, the Supreme Being* and *One Above,* and others with a more precautionary or even ironical flavour, such as *Providence, Fate, Somebody up there,* and perhaps also *Fortune, Luck* and *the lap of the Gods.* A particularly interesting family of terms is the group *It, It all, Things* and *Everything,* which enter into dozens – perhaps hundreds – of idioms. In these idioms *it* seems to indicate the whole of a person's circumstances, considered from a finalizing point of view and as they bear upon her own well-being. Thus we may inquire: 'How are *things*?', How's *it* going?', Is *everything* all right?' And in the main text I have quoted the exchange: 'Is this it? – 'This is *it.*'

From these considerations it is evident that the *It*-group of terms, on examination, could soon be shown to figure in a large number of idioms that have a markedly theological flavour. Their range and variety is as great as we have found in the case of *life*; and at one point *it* is even better than *life*. For when we say: 'This is *it,* the *real thing*!', we posit a kind of divine completeness, a totality, an unsurpassable finality, more clearly than we ever do with the life-idioms. In its flowing contingency, *life* is closer to Being; whereas *it* is perhaps closer to the traditional *God*.

So the question is this: why have I written a life-book, which shows that we now believe in flowing, temporal contingent Be-ing, when I could perhaps equally well have written an it-book, which would have shown that we do still believe in the old God after all?

My reply to this is provisional, for the issues here are deep and call for further enquiry. It is to the effect that the it-idioms are all of them our own expressions. We and we alone do all the talking, and perform all the speech-acts. We posit *it*, and give to *it* all *its* attributes. So whereas life is a pure gift (with no giver), *it* is our construct, and *life* therefore is prior to *it*.

However, more attention to this point will have to wait a while.

* * *

I add a brief note, drawing attention to the strikingly different attitudes of life of two great figures, Dietrich Bonhoeffer and Samuel Beckett.

Beckett seems to have cordially detested the popular life-theology; so much so that he is perhaps the greatest of 'life-atheists'. His characters move in a region where there seems to be no longer any possibility of enjoying or loving life. Some have memories of past happiness, but none have hopes of future happiness. Beckett uses none of the life-idioms and his only significant piece of life-talk, in *Rockaby* (1980), is very short: 'Fuck life'. Much though she loved and admired Beckett, the actress Billie Whitelaw perceptibly found it difficult to say that line – no doubt feeling it to be the ultimate blasphemy, which it is.

In stark contrast, consider Bonhoeffer, writing in his prison letters during the summer of 1944, and with his chances of getting out alive steadily fading. In the most celebrated passages of these letters, the words *live*, *living* and *life* are used with remarkable frequency. Going over them with a highlighter pen, I found myself sometimes using it more than a dozen times a page; and I began to see that Bonhoeffer is attempting to write his protestant faith into the new religious world of 'life'.

In extremis, Beckett is almost the ultimate life-denier and Bonhoeffer almost the ultimate life-affirmer. Which of them do we side with? I am with Bonhoeffer, but it is not easy to disagree with so great a figure as Beckett. I suggest that he joined Schopenhauer in believing that in order to accept death we must first be forced to cut one-by-one every cord by which we are attached to life. I disagree, holding that a fully-religious or 'solar' affirmation of life does not need to be given up in the face of death. It has already 'conquered' death, by including within itself a full acceptance of death. It **has nothing to lose,** and should never be given up.

Notes

Introduction

1. From John Hayward (ed.), *Swift*, London: the Nonesuch Press; New York: Random House 1949, pp.466ff.

2. From Herbert Davis (ed.), *The Prose Works of Jonathan Swift*, Volume IV, Oxford: Basil Blackwell 1957, p.248, where Davis includes the saying as one of the *Thoughts on Various Subjects* jotted down for inclusion in Swift and Pope's *Miscellanies*, 1727. Hayward leaves it out, and so do some other editors; and it is indeed weirdly inconsistent with the *Thought on Religion* quoted above. Swift thought that we are all of us inconsistent beings, and was no doubt well aware of sharply conflicting impulses in himself.

3. C. H. Dodd, *The Interpretation of the Fourth Gospel*, Cambridge: Cambridge University Press 1953, pp.144–150.

1. A New Meaning of 'Life'

1. From *The Doctor's Dilemma* (1906), Act 1.

2. Throughout, the new idioms about life, now recognizably established in common speech, are here printed in **bold** type.

3. Here cited from D. H. Lawrence, *Selected Letters*, Harmondsworth: Penguin Books 1950, p.144.

4. F. R. Leavis, *The Living Principle: English as a Discipline of Thought*, London: Chatto and Windus 1975, pp.205, 263.

5. I quote the words to me of a Cambridge contemporary who is a well-known figure. He's Jewish by birth, but now secular.

6. Gal. 6.10, as cited at the Offertory in the First Prayer Book of 1549, and in all revisions thereafter to 1928.

7. *Ephemera* is Greek for 'of a day', and mayflies, which were traditionally supposed to live for only one day, are called the *Ephemeridae*. The television playwright Dennis Potter is affectionately remembered by the British public for an interview given while he was dying of cancer in which he spoke very eloquently of how beautiful life had come to seem to him.

2. Genealogies of 'Life'

1. *Selected Letters,* cited above, c.1, n.3, p.173 (28 December 1928).

2. From *The Plumed Serpent,* c.XXVI, Penguin edn. of 1950, p.432.

3. Letter to Maria and Aldous Huxley, 9 May 1929; *Selected Letters,* pp.175f.

4. Edition cited above, p.376. From Ramón's open letters to the clergy.

5. Cited from the Library of America omnibus edition of Thoreau's works, New York: Literary Classics of the United States 1985, pp.394f.

6. Ibid., from pp.395f. It is worth reporting also that Thoreau does use the phrase **despair of life**.

7. Ibid., p.394.

8. Cited from a translation by Alastair Reid, reprinted in Jorge Luis Borges, *The Book of Sand,* Harmondsworth: Penguin Books 1979, p.97.

9. Quoted from my *Mysticism After Modernity,* Oxford: Blackwell 1998, p.101. There, I cite from the R. B. Blakney translation of Eckhart, New York: Harper Torchbooks 1957, which has more sayings about life as a self-sourcing end-in-itself on pp.180, 241, 242. The Sermon *In occisione gladii,* pp.170–173, is about God, life and Being.

10. N. K. Sandars, *The Epic of Gilgamesh,* Harmondsworth: Penguin 1972, and later revised edns., p.99.

11. D. H. Lawrence, 'Cypresses'.

12, 13, 14. These three eye-opening quotations are all to be found in J. M. and M. J. Cohen (eds.), *The Penguin Dictionary of Modern Quotations,* second (revised) edn., 1980. See under 'Virginia Woolf' on pp.364ff. The first comes from *The Common Reader,* 1st Series, 'On Not Knowing Greek'; the second, 13, from 'Modern Fiction' in the same volume; and the third is from *Mrs Dalloway.* Taken together, they show that Virginia Woolf's religious feeling for life must have been as highly-developed as Lawrence's.

There are, however, considerable differences between the two writers. Lawrence uses the word 'life' with a rushing hectic religious eloquence, and would not dream of pausing to explain it. Woolf, in the four volumes of her posthumously-published *Collected Essays,* quite often puts 'life' in quotation marks in order to remind us to pause and think what a queer wide-ranging word it is. She can, as in the essay on 'The Death of the Moth', use it in the old approximately-Schopenhauerian sense of the Will-to-Live, a force of nature, cosmic energy. But more often she is using it to signify the rather-elusive thing that modern fiction is trying to be about: the flux of goings-on, relations and exchanges in the human life-world. She wonders why it is that mere accurate reportage cannot make a novel live: why is such a huge artistic effort needed in order to create a convincing effect? She almost has a *Negative Bio-theology* of **real life** – the thing that everybody feels so sure of, and yet so few of us can deliver in writing. See, further, c.5, below.

15. For this whole paragraph, see *The Living Principle* (cited c.1, note 4), Part 3: 'Four Quartets'.

16. For Schopenhauer's influence, see Bryan Magee, *The Philosophy of Schopenhauer,* Oxford: the Clarendon Press 1983, Appendices 1–8, pp.245–393. Magee finds in Dylan Thomas's

The force that through the green fuse drives the flower
Drives my green age . . .

a vivid echo of a passage in Schopenhauer: pp.391ff.

17. Cited here from Douglas Grant (ed.), *Dryden: Poetry Prose and Plays*, London: Rupert Hart-Davies 1952, p.398.

18. Ibid., p.484.

19. Ibid., p.485.

20. From Johnson's Preface to *The Plays of William Shakespeare,* here cited from Donald Greene (ed.), *Samuel Johnson,* in the Oxford Authors series, Oxford: Oxford University Press 1984, p.421.

21. A friend recommends me to consider the writings of certain Italian Humanists on the subject of human life, human dignity and human freedom. The standard survey of these writers is Charles Trinkhaus, *In our Image and Likeness: Humanity and Divinity in Italian Humanist Thought*, in two volumes, London: Constable 1970. The chief texts are Marsilio Ficino (1433–99), *Theologica platonica* (1482), and the later *Libri de vita*; and Giovanni Pico della Mirandola (1463–94), *Oratio de hominis dignitate* (c.1486). Ficino develops the doctrine that 'man is made in the image of God' in the direction of ascribing divinity to man; Pico della Mirandola, in a famous passage, says that our dignity lies in the fact that we don't have a fully-determinate and ready-made nature, but have been left by God to make of ourselves what we wish. However, I don't find in either of these writers quite the new and very remarkable notion of life, as an object rather like Heidegger's 'Being', which concerns me in this book.

22. Mention of Luther's alleged table-talk prompts me to air an hypothesis about the historical origin of the modern sense of life as *libido*, a universal vitalizing power immanent within us that is a little distinct from us. Luther's saying is to the effect that the Pope established his rule over everything, but there was one small part of man's body that not even the Pope could enslave, and that small part rose up and overthrew him.

Luther's idea here is derived from Christian Platonism and especially from St Augustine. (See *The City of God*, Books 13 and 14, and especially 14, chap. 26.) It was held in antiquity, and especially by the Platonists, that reason should be sovereign over all parts of the body and in all the affairs of life. Any convulsive, non-rational motion of the body seemed to be a symptom of sickness, sin or demonic influence. Thus St Paul, in Romans

7.23, says that if a part of the body behaves **as if it has a life of its own**, and is not subject to 'the law of my mind', then it makes me 'captive to the law of sin'. Developing this idea, Augustine was led to the view that the erection of the male organ was a symptom of the Fall. Unfallen human beings, Adam and Eve, had copulated in Paradise in a purely rational manner, without the erection of the male organ – and, we gather, without any difficulty. In addition, theologians already knew on other grounds that Original Sin is transmitted in the male line, along with everything else in us that is hereditary (Hebrews 7.4–10).

Thus the connection of the male sex drive and the erection of the male organ with Original Sin – and therefore, symbolically, a connection of life *itself* with original sin – is very deeply rooted in Latin Christian thought. Readers of Boccaccio will recall a story in which the erect penis is referred to (by a priest) as 'the Devil'. And Luther's bawdy table talk (whether apocryphal or not) belongs in a Renaissance world of thought in which, for the first time, the sex drive is just beginning to be revalued and seen as a liberating force, affirming life and heathily refusing to be kept locked up.

Schopenhauer, with his doctrine that 'the Will' expresses itself in us most explicitly in the genitals and the sex drive, stands in the same old Western tradition. He remains lugubrious and pessimistic, trying to gain happiness by denying the Will and denying life. Nietzsche tries to say Yes to life, but never quite managed to say Yes to sex. Lawrence does better, but even today our film and TV censors continue to regard the erect male organ as the most obscene thing of all.

If I am right in saying that today a dramatic religious revaluation of life is taking place, it must include a revaluation of the sex drive – and not least, on the part of men. And perhaps there is evidence that this is happening.

23. In English grammar schools during the last years of the Middle Ages the use of the vernacular during school hours was forbidden, and pupils were encouraged to inform upon each other for using it. Nevertheless, the vernacular gradually asserted itself, as at Long Melford, where it is built into the physical fabric of the church.

At Long Melford, too, the saints in the stained glass windows have been replaced by the well-to-do merchants and their wives whose money paid for the building. Here the secular and sacred worlds are already beginning to flow together.

24. On this, see a very good essay by Thomas J. J. Altizer, 'The Atheistic Ground of America', in William J. Hynes and William Dean (eds.), *American Religious Empiricism: Working Papers: Vol. 1*, Regis College Press 1988, pp.97–112.

25. On the meaning of the early history of religion, see Marcel Gauchet, *The Disenchantment of the World: A political history of religion*, Princeton NJ: Princeton University Press 1998, and my *After God: The*

future of religion, London: Weidenfeld and Nicholson 1997.

26. See my *The Religion of Being*, London: SCM Press 1998.

27. 'Burnt Norton', V.

28. Gilles Deleuze, *Bergsonism*, New York: Zone Books 1988, explains Bergson's idea of life through the ideas of duration, memory and *élan vital*.

3. Ways of Relating Oneself to Life

1. *Bionomous* is a coinage, and a variant of Paul Tillich's term *theonomous*. See his *Systematic Theology*, Volume 1, London: Nisbet 1953, pp.92–96. Theonomy is defined by Tillich as 'autonomous reason united with its own ground', p.94. *Bionomy* then consists in language's turning back upon itself and relating itself humorously to the outpouring life-energy that powers it, sustains it, and indeed *is* its own better half.

2. I used rather similar imagery in the two 1998 books about Being, for the same reasons. After I had completed the Being-books it struck me that if I changed my vocabulary yet again and rethought everything in terms of the relation to Life, I would find that ordinary language has already done most of the work for me. Instead of the usual struggle to communicate ideas that normal people find pretty deplorable, I'd be in the happy position of being able to say: 'Look! This is what you are already saying; this is what you already think'. Isn't it?

3. 'The Death of the Moth' is a short essay that gives its title to the first volume of Virginia Woolf's essays to be published after her death by Leonard Woolf (1942). I quote here from the four-volume *Collected Essays*, London: Hogarth Press 1966, Volume 1, pp.359–361.

4. Ibid., p.359.

5. Ibid., p.360.

6. Ibid., p.361.

7. Deuteronomy 30.19.

8. For Kierkegaard on anxiety, see especially *The Concept of Anxiety* (1844), tr. Reidar Thomte and Albert B. Anderson, Kierkegaard's Writings, Vol. VIII, New Jersey: Princeton University Press 1981,; and *The Anxieties of the Heathen: Christian Discourses* (1848), tr. Walter Lowrie and printed in *Christian Discourses*, New York: Oxford University Press 1961. The discourses on the anxieties of the heathen are sermons on Matthew 6.24–34.

9. *The Concept of Anxiety*, edition cited above, p.43.

10. Ibid., supplement, p.170.

11. E.g., Romans 7.

12. Flagstad could even be self-stigmatizing. A friend reported seeing the palms of her hands with blood on them after a performance. She had clenched her fists so tightly while singing that her fingernails dug into her palms.

4. Bio-theology

1. From William Blake.

2. From the D. H. Lawrence letter of 29 September 1922, cited above, c.1, note 3.

3. '(Nietzsche) never got a life outside literature'; in 'Derrida and the Philosophical Tradition'; reprinted in *Truth and Progress: Philosophical Papers, Volume 3*, Cambridge and New York: Cambridge University Press 1998, p.327.

4. Horatio Bottomley, speech to the Oxford Union, 2 December 1920: 'Gentlemen, I have not had your advantages. What poor education I have received has been gained in the university of life'.

5. Schweitzer hoped to be remembered, not primarily as organist, or medical missionary or theologian, but as a post-Nietzschean philosopher of *Kultur* and of life. But even more than Lawrence, he is now profoundly unfashionable even while his ideas are prevailing. See George Seaver, *Albert Schweitzer: The Man and his Mind*, London: A. and C. Black 1947, c.XVII: 'The Ethic of Reverence for Life'. The key book is the *Civilization and Ethics*, which forms the second 'book' of *The Philosophy of Civilization*, New York: Macmillan 1981.

6. The Hebrew Bible is traditionally divided into three parts: the Law, the Prophets, and the Writings. Orthodox rabbinic Judaism concentrates its attention upon the first of these, the Torah, *the Law* of Moses. Christianity has especially admired *the Prophets* (which include all the major historical books), because the themes of a national history of salvation and the entry of the divine Word into history contributed to much to its own classical theology of itself as the new Israel, the City of God, the Church Militant.

This present book suggests that the theology of the future should build much more upon the *Writings* – the various poetical books and collections of Wisdom-sayings. For as Walter Bruggeman and other scholars have observed, there are similarities between ancient wisdom and our post-modern sense of 'life'. Wisdom was relatively indifferent to ideas of special election, divine protection, and final salvation. It was notably international. Like us, it tended to see the human world as just going on, without any hidden hand or final resolution.

Some scholars nowadays present Jesus as a teacher of Wisdom. He was not notably ethnocentric. Sometimes his teaching seems to envisage a completion of human life in the eternal realm, but at other times he sees human life as being completed here just in our own wholehearted and faithful commitment to it, and in certain epiphanic moments of joy.

5. *But what is Life?*

1. See the last sentence of c.XVI, 'Recapitulation and Conclusion', in all editions.

2. And a surge of public interest in reading popular science books. The pop science writer has – for the moment, at least – replaced both the philosopher and the theologian.

3. The century was first popularized by a group of early Lutheran church historians, the Magdeburg Centuriators, who published at Basel (1559–1574) a church history divided by centuries.

4. Paraphrased from II Peter 3.8; compare Ps. 90.4 and Ecclus. 18.10. Similar statements about Brahman abound in the Hindu tradition. It is worth remarking, by the way, that early in the Vedic writings there was a school of thought that made 'breath' or life the ultimate cosmological principle. See R. C. Zaehner, *Hinduism*, London: Oxford University Press 1962, c.II, 'Brahman', pp.47–64.

5. Ray Monk, *Ludwig Wittgenstein: The Duty of Genius*, London: Jonathan Cape 1990.

6. *Collected Essays*, ed. Leonard Woolf, 1966, Volume 2, p.105.

7. Ibid

8. Ibid, p.106.

9. Ibid., p.107.

10. Ibid., p.109.

11. All these phrases are taken from the same volume, pp.135f.

12. At this point contrast Virginia Woolf's views about the novel and about life with those of E. M. Forster, in his *Aspects of the Novel*, London: Edward Arnold 1927. Woolf's review of the book, written in the same year, is reprinted in her *Collected Essays*, Volume 2, pp.51–58, under the title 'The Art of Fiction', written in 1927. Forster is anti-theoretical, a British empiricist and a secular humanist who wants his stories to be true to life. He regards *Ulysses* as a fantasy, and also 'far more than a fantasy – it is a dogged attempt to cover the universe with mud, an inverted Victorianism, an attempt to make crossness and dirt succeed where sweetness and light failed . . .' (p.113). In short, Forster is secular and philistine; and Woolf remarks that he does not discuss language. Nor does he attempt to trace life to its source within us. Woolf, despite her gentility, is well able to appreciate Joyce's greatness. She is religious, in a sense in which Forster is not.

13. See *Study of Thomas Hardy and Other Essays*, ed. Bruce Steele, in the Cambridge Edition of the Works of D. H. Lawrence, Cambridge University Press 1985. My quotations are drawn from chapters III and IV.

14. Ibid., p.29.

15. Ibid., p.39.

16. Ibid., p.35.

17. Ibid.

18. T. M. Knox and Richard Kroner (eds), *On Christianity: Early Theological Writings by Friedrich Hegel*, New York: Harper Torchbooks 1961, p.255.

19. Ibid., p.254.

20. In more detail, everything in history is historically explicable: scientists, scientific work and the whole body of scientific knowledge all of them within history; *therefore* they all, together with their historical changes, are historically explicable.

Thus science is in principle completely explicable by historians of science, just as all religious ideas and institutions are also in principle historically explicable. It is as wrong to expect the academic discipline called History of Science to lend ideological support to popular scientific realism as it is to expect Church History to lend ideological support to popular dogmatic realism.

6. *Life, Being and God*

1. On Spinoza's religious naturalism, there is now Richard Mason, *The God of Spinoza: a philosophical study*, Cambridge: Cambridge University Press 1997. Spinoza's system already shows very clearly that to secularize religion by bringing God down into the world, or 'life', is thereby also to divinize Nature, or 'life'. How can Christians object to such a move? Isn't it what their religion is meant to be about?

2. Colin Crowder (ed), *God and Reality: Essays on Christian Non-Realism*, London and New York: Mowbray/Cassell 1997, p.24.

3. Buddhist demythologizers include Stephen Batchelor, *Buddhism Without Beliefs: A Contemporary Guide to Awakening*, New York: Riverhead Books/G. P. Putnam's 1997, and R.S. Bucknell and Martin Stuart-Fox, *The Twilight Language: Explorations in Buddhist Meditation and Symbolism*, Richmond, Surrey: Curzon Press 1993.

4. For a good recent example of tightrope-walking, see L. Wittgenstein, *Culture and Value*, Oxford: Blackwell 1980, p.73.

5. The Venerable Bede, *The Ecclesiastical History of the English Nation* Book II, c.13, cited here from the Everyman edition of 1910, p.91.

6. **Is That It?** was used as a book-title by Bob Geldof (1986). **This is It** was used by Alan Watts (1958) – quite an early date for the phrase, *and* for his recognition of its religious force.

Index of Names